D0153930

POLITICAL AGENDAS FOR EDUCATION

"This is a must book for any professor teaching educational policy. Spring's analyses are insightful and balanced in presentation among the competing social-political forces. The insights offered are unparalleled in the sheer specificity he offers his readers."
—Rosemary Papa, Northern Arizona University, USA

"An excellent resource for giving students a quick reference to political agendas and positions within the national political scene in America especially related to education."
—Jim Johnson, Point Loma Nazarene University, USA

The Fifth Edition of Joel Spring's ongoing documentation and analysis of political agendas for education reflects the major political issues in education since 2008. This edition focuses on the education sections of the 2012 Republican, Democratic, Green, and Libertarian Party platforms. Taking a fresh look at the social and political forces, educational research, and ideologies shaping the educational agendas of these political parties and a comparative approach, the book stimulates reflection and discussion.

New coverage in the Fifth Edition includes:

- The political coup called Race to the Top
- Common Core State Standards and national testing based on the Standards
- Explosion of online instruction
- Debates about teacher evaluations and merit pay
- Growing for-profit education industry
- New Agenda for American Education: Constitutional amendment; long life and happiness; environmental education

Political Agendas for Education is essential reading for courses dealing with the politics of education, foundations of education, educational leadership, and curriculum studies, and for educational scholars, professionals, policymakers, and all those concerned with the politics of education in the U.S. and its consequences for schools and society.

Joel Spring is Professor at Queens College/City University of New York and the Graduate Center of the City University of New York, USA.

Sociocultural, Political, and Historical Studies in Education
Joel Spring, Editor

Gabbard, Ed. • *Knowledge and Power in the Global Economy: The Effects of School Reform in a Neoliberal/Neoconservative Age, Second Edition*

Spring • *A New Paradigm for Global School Systems: Education for a Long and Happy Life*

Books, Ed. • *Invisible Children in the Society and Its Schools, Third Edition*

Spring • *Pedagogies of Globalization: The Rise of the Educational Security State*

Sidhu • *Universities and Globalization: To Market, To Market*

Bowers/Apffel-Marglin, Eds. • *Rethinking Freire: Globalization and the Environmental Crisis*

Reagan • *Non-Western Educational Traditions: Indigenous Approaches to Educational Thought and Practice, Third Edition*

Books • *Poverty and Schooling in the U.S.: Contexts and Consequences*

Shapiro/Purpel, Eds. • *Critical Social Issues in American Education: Democracy and Meaning in a Globalizing World, Third Edition*

Spring • *How Educational Ideologies are Shaping Global Society: Intergovernmental Organizations, NGOs, and the Decline of the Nation-State*

Lakes/Carter, Eds. • *Global Education for Work: Comparative Perspectives on Gender and the New Economy*

Heck • *Studying Educational and Social Policy: Theoretical Concepts and Research Methods*

Peshkin • *Places of Memory: Whiteman's Schools and Native American Communities*

Hemmings • *Coming of Age in U.S. High Schools: Economic, Kinship, Religious, and Political Crosscurrents*

Spring • *Educating the Consumer-Citizen: A History of the Marriage of Schools, Advertising, and Media*

Ogbu • *Black American Students in an Affluent Suburb: A Study of Academic Disengagement*

Benham/Stein, Eds. • *The Renaissance of American Indian Higher Education: Capturing the Dream*

Hones, Ed. • *American Dreams, Global Visions: Dialogic Teacher Research with Refugee and Immigrant Families*

McCarty • *A Place to Be Navajo: Rough Rock and The Struggle for Self-Determination in Indigenous Schooling*

Spring • *Globalization and Educational Rights: An Intercivilizational Analysis*

Grant/Lei, Eds. • *Global Constructions of Multicultural Education: Theories and Realities*

Luke • *Globalization and Women in Academics: North/West–South/East*

Meyer/Boyd, Eds. • *Education Between State, Markets, and Civil Society: Comparative Perspectives*

Roberts • *Remaining and Becoming: Cultural Crosscurrents in an Hispano School*

Borman/Stringfield/Slavin, Eds. • *Title I: Compensatory Education at the Crossroads*

DeCarvalho • *Rethinking Family-School Relations: A Critique of Parental Involvement in Schooling*

Peshkin • *Permissible Advantage?: The Moral Consequences of Elite Schooling*

For additional information on titles in the Sociocultural, Political, and Historical Studies in Education series visit **www.routledge.com/education**

POLITICAL AGENDAS FOR EDUCATION

From Race to the Top to Saving the Planet

Fifth Edition

Joel Spring

Routledge
Taylor & Francis Group

NEW YORK AND LONDON

Fifth edition published 2014
by Routledge
711 Third Avenue, New York, NY 10017

And in the UK
by Routledge
2 Park Square, Milton Park, Abingdon, Oxon OX14 4RN

Routledge is an imprint of the Taylor & Francis Group, an informa business

© 2014 Taylor & Francis

The right of Joel Spring to be identified as author of this work has been asserted
by him in accordance with sections 77 and 78 of the Copyright, Designs and
Patents Act 1988.

All rights reserved. No part of this book may be reprinted or reproduced or
utilised in any form or by any electronic, mechanical, or other means, now known
or hereafter invented, including photocopying and recording, or in any
information storage or retrieval system, without permission in writing from
the publishers.

Trademark notice: Product or corporate names may be trademarks or registered
trademarks, and are used only for identification and explanation without intent to
infringe.

First edition published 1997 by Routledge
Fourth edition published 2009 by Routledge

Library of Congress Cataloging in Publication Data
Spring, Joel H.
   Political agendas for education: from race to the top to saving the planet /
by Joel Spring. — Fifth edition.
      pages cm. — (Sociocultural, political, and historical studies in education)
   Includes bibliographical references and index.
   1. Education—Political aspects—United States.   2. Liberalism—United
States.   3. Conservatism—United States.   I. Title.
   LC89.S663 2013+
   379.73—dc23   2013021772

ISBN: 978-0-415-82814-7 (hbk)
ISBN: 978-0-415-82815-4 (pbk)
ISBN: 978-0-203-48689-4 (ebk)

Typeset in Bembo
by RefineCatch Limited, Bungay, Suffolk, UK

Printed and bound in Great Britain by TJ International Ltd, Padstow, Cornwall

CONTENTS

PREFACE

A central focus of the Fifth Edition of *Political Agendas for Education* is the Race to the Top. In Chapter 1, "Democrats for Education Reform: Race to the Top," I discuss the role of Democrats for Education Reform in supplying President Barack Obama and his Secretary of Education Arne Duncan with the ideas and policies for Race to the Top. In Chapter 2, "The Political Coup Known as Race to the Top," I discuss the ideology of those supporting Race to the Top, the benefits reaped by for-profit companies from its policies, the influence of Teach For America, and how these policies have allowed for increased economic and racial segregation.

Republican reaction and rejection of Race to the Top is discussed in Chapter 3, "The Republican Party, Race to the Top, and Choice." This chapter includes a discussion of the Republican National Committee's statement criticizing the Obama education agenda. Also, in Chapter 3, I discuss Republican efforts to expand school choice through vouchers and the use of debit cards. The Republican social agenda for schools is discussed in Chapter 4, "The Republican Education Agenda: The Culture Wars." The Republican social agenda includes concerns about abortion, gay marriage, abstinence education, evolution, and school prayer.

In Chapter 5, "Green and Libertarian Party Agendas," I discuss two minority parties that are the harshest critics of the Republican and Democratic education agendas. The Green Party calls for repealing No Child Left Behind and returning schools to local community control. The Green Party's education agenda emphasizes educating students for civic activism and environmental sustainability. Art education, an important part of the Green Party agenda, is seen as a means of unmasking oppression and imagining solutions to economic and social problems. Libertarians call for separation of school and state by turning over education to the free market and phasing out the involvement of government.

In Chapter 6, "New Agenda for American Schools," I bring together proposals I have made in different contexts. One is a proposal for an amendment to the U.S. Constitution that would ensure equal funding of public schools, academic freedom for teachers, local control of schools, and protection of languages of culture. My other proposal replaces the current human capital emphasis on education for work and growing the economy with a new goal of educating for a long and satisfying life. And finally, I call for a renewed emphasis on environmental education as an important part of educating students for a long life and happiness.

1

DEMOCRATS FOR EDUCATION REFORM

Race to the Top

Senator Barack Obama's dinner in 2005 at the Café Gray in the New York City's Time Warner building dramatically changed the Democratic Party's education agenda. The dinner was hosted by a group of investment bankers organized as Democrats for Education Reform which had declared its goal of returning "the Democratic Party to its rightful place as a champion of children, first and foremost, in America's public education systems."[1] The work of this group resulted in current "school reform" proposals contained in Obama's Race to the Top—creating a common core state curriculum, teacher evaluations using student test scores, and the expansion of charter schools. Democrats for Education Reform also played an important role in President Obama's selection of Arne Duncan as U.S. Secretary of Education.[2]

After the dinner at the Café Gray, Senator Obama and the Democrats for Education Reform went to the apartment of one founder of the group, Boykin Curry, who is associated with the investment group Eagle Capital and a cofounder of Public Prep, a nonprofit charter school company operating schools in New York City with the mission of developing "single-sex elementary and middle public schools that pursue excellence through continuous learning and data-driven instruction."[3] Before a group of about 150 people at Curry's apartment, it was reported, Senator Obama stood on a chair and, among other things, told the gathering, "If someone can tell me where the Democratic Party stands on education reform, please let me know. Because I can't figure it out. Our Party has got to wake up on this."[4]

After his election in 2008, President Obama announced the education initiative Race to the Top, in which states competed for federal funds to implement what was mainly the proposals of the Democrats for Education Reform. Each part of the Race to the Top agenda was assigned specific points which a state received if their proposals reflected the federal administrations education agenda. For example, the Race to the Top agenda specified, and these are only three examples, the following points to be added to a total state score:

1. Developing and implementing common, high-quality assessments (10 points).
2. Ensuring successful conditions for high-performing charter schools and other innovative schools (40 points).
3. Improving teacher and principal effectiveness based on performance (58 points).[5]

President Obama's Secretary of Education, Arne Duncan, in describing the criteria to be used to award federal funds under Race to the Top, declared:

> States, for example, that limit *alternative routes to certification* for teachers and principals, or cap the number of *charter schools*, will be at a competitive disadvantage. And states that explicitly prohibit *linking data on achievement or student growth to principal and teacher evaluations* will be ineligible for reform dollars until they change their laws [author's emphasis].[6]

Questioning Democratic Education Goals

Race to the Top attempts to achieve traditional Democratic goals of reducing poverty and income inequalities, and making the U.S. the number one global economy. Can education solve economic problems or do economic problems create educational inequalities? This question is fundamental to analyzing the Democratic education agenda. For instance, is the statement true in the 2008 Democratic platform, "In the 21st Century, where the most valuable skill is knowledge, countries that out-educate us today will out-compete us tomorrow"?[7] Or is the claim true in the 2012 Democratic platform that "getting an education is the surest path to the middle class, giving all students the opportunity to fulfill their dreams and contribute to our economy and democracy"?[8] It might seem heretical to question these claims, but there are problems in causality in trying to tie education to economic goals.

Since the 1960s, as I discuss in more detail later in the chapter, Democrats made the claim of a close connection between education, poverty, and economic growth. One question about this connection is whether low-quality schooling causes poverty and income inequalities or are these primarily caused by other factors, such as the availability of jobs, the tax structure, or decisions made by corporations? Is improved education the key to global economic competition or is it other factors, such as the movement of companies and jobs to other countries or the failure to invest in infrastructure?

In addition, there are no longitudinal research studies that the economy will improve, poverty and income inequalities will be reduced, and the U.S. will be more competitive in the global economic system as a result of a reform agenda based on Common Core State Standards, expanding charter schools, expanding public preschool education, and evaluating teachers using students' test scores. It is even questionable as to whether longitudinal research can be designed to show these connections given all the other social, political, and economic factors that influence the world's economies.

What can be said for sure is that research has not been done on the long term economic consequences of the Democratic education reform agenda, since the impact of these educational changes will occur sometime in the future. In other words, this education agenda is being put in place without any proof that it will achieve its objectives. There is no research, and again it may be impossible to design a longitudinal research study, that shows any relationship between the Common Core State Standards and improving America's ability to compete in the global economy despite the fact that the mission statement of the Common Core State Curriculum claims:

> The Common Core State Standards ... are designed to be robust and relevant to the real world, reflecting the knowledge and skills that our young people need for success in college and careers. With American students fully prepared for the future, our communities will be best positioned to compete successfully in the global economy.[9]

Is this the reality?

While there is research that some charter schools can raise test scores, there is no research that shows charter schools will reduce poverty and income inequalities and make the U.S. more competitive in world economies. There are no studies showing that evaluating teachers based on student test scores will improve the economy. However, there is longitudinal research, which I describe later, that preschool will improve the ability of children from low-income families to be employed and stay out of jail.

Simply stated, despite claims of human capital economists, there is no research that convincingly shows changing schools will improve America's ability to compete in world markets. The ability to compete in global markets may be a function of other economic factors and not education. In fact, the U.S. and China now face the problem of too many college graduates, which has resulted in educational inflation or the declining economic value of a college degree. *The New York Times* reporter Catherine Rampell, in an article with the descriptive title, "It Takes a B.A. to Find a Job as a File Clerk," writes, "The college degree is becoming the new high school diploma: the new minimum requirement, albeit an expensive one, for getting even the lowest-level job."[10] Regarding China, *The New York Times* reporter Keith Bradsher wrote regarding family struggles to ensure their child receives a college education, "Yet a college degree no longer ensures a well-paying job, because the number of graduates in China has quadrupled in the last decade."[11]

Democrats, Education, Poverty, and Elementary and Secondary Education Act

Since the 1960s War on Poverty, the Democratic Party has pursued federal policies to end inequality of educational opportunity and equality of economic opportunity. Since the 1990s, Democrats claimed improving the school system was key to improving America's economic system in global markets. In 2001, both Democrats and Republicans sponsored amendments to the 1965 Elementary and Secondary Education Act (ESEA), which became known as the No Child Left Behind Act of 2001 (signed into law on January 8, 2002), which had the stated purpose of "Improving the Academic Achievement of the Disadvantaged."[12] Regarding the global economy, when Democratic President Bill Clinton ran in 1992 the Democratic platform declared: "A competitive American economy requires the global market's best educated, best trained, most flexible work force."[13]

The War on Poverty was launched during Democratic President Lyndon Johnson's administration (November 22, 1963–January 20, 1969). The most important education legislation of the period was Title I of the 1965 ESEA.

Title I of ESEA, signed by President Johnson on April 11, 1965, provided funds for improved educational programs for children designated as "educationally deprived." Title I of the 1965 legislation:

> declares it to be the policy of the United States to provide financial assistance . . . to expand and improve . . . educational programs by various means . . . which contribute particularly to meeting the special educational needs of educationally deprived children.[14]

Rather than "deprived children," the later renamed 2001 legislation, No Child Left Behind, uses the term "disadvantaged" and opens, "TITLE I—IMPROVING THE ACADEMIC ACHIEVEMENT OF THE DISADVANTAGED."[15]

The War on Poverty was announced on January 8, 1964 by Democratic President Lyndon Johnson in his State of the Union message to Congress. He told Congress that it was the federal government's responsibility to replace despair with opportunity and he said, "this administration today, here and now, declares unconditional war on poverty in America."[16] In January 1965, President Johnson announced funding of the preschool program Head Start as part of the federal government's antipoverty program. Head Start was launched in the summer of 1965 under the supervision of the Office of Economic Opportunity.

Title I, along with the preschool program Head Start, were the major educational components of the War on Poverty. At the opening of congressional hearings on ESEA, Secretary of Health, Education, and Welfare Anthony J. Celebrezze and Commissioner of Education Francis Keppel provided the President's justification and rationale for special educational assistance to the "educationally deprived." In his opening statement to the committee, Celebrezze quoted President Johnson's statement, "Just as ignorance breeds poverty, poverty all too often breeds ignorance in the next generation." Celebrezze went on to claim, "The President's program . . . is designed to break this cycle which has been running on from generation to generation in this most affluent period of our history." He stated that a clear link exists between high educational attainment and high economic attainment.[17]

Support for Secretary Celebrezze's argument was contained in a highly influential 1964 report by Walter Heller, chairman of the President's Council of Economic Advisors.

A section in the Council's annual report titled "The Problem of Poverty in America," gave education a central role in combating poverty: "Equality of opportunity is the American dream, and universal education our noblest pledge to realize it. But, for the children of the poor, education is a handicap race; many are too ill motivated at home to learn at school." Also, the report claimed, "The chief reason for low rates of pay is low productivity, which in turn can reflect lack of education or training, physical and mental disability, or poor motivation."[18]

The Heller report linked education and poverty: "The importance of education as a factor in poverty is suggested by the fact that families headed by persons with no more than 8 years of education have an incidence rate [poverty] of 37 percent." Arguing education of children from low-income families was the key to ending poverty, the report stressed the importance of preschool education: "This often means that schooling must start on a pre-school basis and include a broad range of more intensive services."[19]

A major source of the War on Poverty arguments that education, including preschool, could reduce poverty originated in the work of economists Theodore Shultz and Gary Becker.[20] In 1961, Theodore Shultz stated, "economists have long known that people are an important part of the wealth of nations."[21] He argued that people invested in education to improve their job opportunities. In a similar fashion, nations could invest to increase educational opportunities as a stimulus for economic growth. In his original 1964 book on human capital, Gary Becker asserted that economic growth now depended on the knowledge, information, ideas, skills, and health of the workforce. Investments in education, he argued, could improve human capital which would contribute to economic growth.[22] Later, he used the term *knowledge* economy: "An economy like that of the United States is called a capitalist economy, but the more accurate term is human capital or *knowledge* capital economy."[23] Becker claimed that human capital represented three-fourths of the wealth of the U.S. and that investment in education would be the key to further economic growth.[24]

After the 1960s, the Democratic Party continued to campaign for preschool education as a means of achieving equality of educational opportunity. The 1968 campaign platform—the Democrats lost the presidency to Richard Nixon in the election—promised: "We will marshal our national resources to help develop and finance new and effective methods of dealing with the educationally disadvantaged—including expanded preschool programs to prepare all young children for full participation in formal education."[25] The platform also declared: "The new pre-school program known as Head Start has proven its effectiveness in widening the horizons of over two million poor children and their parents."[26]

In the 1972 election, the Democratic Party took the bold step of advocating universal child care programs as part of its "Rights of Children." The platform declared: "We call for the federal government to fund comprehensive development child care programs that will be family centered, locally controlled and universally available." The Democrats included early childhood education and health services in the proposal, calling for universal child care: "Health, social service and early childhood education should be part of these programs, as well as a variety of options most appropriate to their needs."[27]

The Democratic Party continued to support federal child care programs and Head Start in their failed campaigns for the presidency against Ronald Reagan. When President Bill Clinton was elected in 1992, the Democratic Party maintained its support for Head Start and child care: "To help children reach school ready to learn, we will expand child health and nutrition programs and extend Head Start to all eligible children, and guarantee all children access to quality, affordable child care."[28] The 2000 Democratic platform referred to new research showing that, "High-quality preschool should no longer be a luxury. Research ... shows that giving kids a smart start can lead to higher reading and achievement levels, higher graduation rates, and greater success in the workplace."[29] The 2004 Democratic platform supported preschool education: "Because education in the earliest years of a child's life is critical, we will expand and improve preschool and Head Start initiatives with the goal of offering these opportunities to all children."[30]

The emphasis on preschool as a poverty reduction program continued into President Obama's administration. In the 2008 Democratic platform's section "Poverty," it was stated, "Working together, *we can cut poverty in half within ten years.* We will provide all our children a world-class education, from *early childhood through college* [author's emphasis]."[31] In his 2013 State of the Union address, Democratic President Obama stressed preschool education:

> And for poor kids who need help the most, this lack of access to pre-school education can shadow them for the rest of their lives. So, tonight, I propose working with states to make high-quality preschool available to every single child in America. Every dollar we invest in high-quality early childhood education can save more than seven dollars later on, by boosting graduation rates, reducing teen pregnancy, even reducing violent crime.[32]

Democrats for Education Reform: Continuing the War on Poverty

Continuing to advocate education as an economic cure-all, the Democrats for Education Reform broke with traditional Democratic political alliances by asserting that teachers' unions and the school establishment were a major source of educational inequalities. The group's "Statement of Principles" asserts:

> These systems [public schools], once viewed romantically as avenues of opportunity for all, have become captive to powerful, entrenched interests that too often put the demands of adults before the educational needs of children. This perverse hierarchy of priorities is political, and thus requires a political response.[33]

Who were these "entrenched interests"? According to the Democrats for Education Reform, they were teachers' unions, local and state public school bureaucracies, and teacher training institutions. These "entrenched interests," according to the group, were hindering the ability to:

1. evaluate and fire poor teachers and to establish alternative pathways to teacher certification: "All states and districts should begin moving immediately to create teacher evaluation systems comprised of multiple measures that are part a single statewide assessment of teacher effectiveness";[34]
2. provide greater parental school choice by expanding public charter schools: "We support mechanisms that allow parents to select excellent schools for their children, and where education dollars follow each child to their school";[35]
3. create national curriculum standards: "We support clearly-articulated national standards and expectations for core subject areas, while allowing states and local districts to determine how best to make sure that all students are reaching those standards" and "We support policies which stimulate the creation of new, accountable public schools and which simultaneously close down failing schools";[36]
4. establish mayoral control of schools: "We support governance structures which hold leaders responsible, while giving them the tools to effectuate change. We believe in empowering mayors to lead urban school districts, so that they can be held accountable by the electorate."[37]

Like previous Democrats, Democrats for Education Reform wanted to reduce educational inequalities:

> A first-rate system of public education is the cornerstone of a prosperous, free and just society, yet millions of American children today – particularly

low-income and children of color – are trapped in persistently failing schools that are part of deeply dysfunctional school systems.[38]

Democrats for Education Reform: Quality Teachers and the Unions

An explosive issue for Democrats and their longtime allies, the teacher unions, were proposals for using student test scores to evaluate teachers. Traditionally, the two teachers' unions, the National Education Association and the American Federation of Teachers, supported the Democratic Party while being criticized by the Republican Party. For instance, in 2004 Republican President George W. Bush's Secretary of Education Rod Paige called the National Education Association, largest of the two teachers' unions, a terrorist organization. Paige portrayed union reactions as a firestorm.[39] Using the loaded term "terrorist," Paige's comment reflected the traditional animosity Republicans felt towards the two teachers' unions.

Teacher union support of the Democratic Party began during the administration of President Ronald Reagan (1980–1987) when he threatened to abolish the U.S. Department of Education. During Reagan's second year in office, *Education Week*'s Eileen White reported, "The National Education Association (NEA), which has seen its political fortunes suffer during the first year of the Reagan Administration, is once again on the offensive."[40] The union organized its 1.7 million members to combat "the decline of the federal role in education."[41]

Teacher union support of the Democratic Party continued to President Obama's administration. Republican hostility towards the two unions persisted as exemplified by the title of U.S. Secretary of Education Rod Paige's 2006 book *The War Against Hope: How Teachers' Unions Hurt Children, Hinder Teachers, and Endanger Public Education*. Splashed across the back of the book's dust cover was the warning: "Without question, the greatest impediment to meaningful school reform is the enormous, self-aggrandizing power wielded by the teachers' unions."[42]

The Democrats for Education Reform put the Democratic Party in conflict with the teachers' unions by calling for changes in teacher tenure, credentialing, and merit pay. Reflecting this changed focus was the influential 2006 Brooking Institute's Hamilton Project report *Identifying Effective Teachers Using Performance on the Job*.[43]

The Hamilton Project report dismissed traditional methods of teacher credentialing involving simply taking a specified set of college courses and passing a test. The report cited studies that showed there was little difference in quality between credentialed and non-credentialed teachers. As a result, the report advocated increasing alternative routes to teaching:[44]

Recommendation 1: Reduce the barriers to entry into teaching for those without traditional teacher certification. The evidence suggests that there is no reason to limit initial entrance into teaching to those who have completed traditional certification programs or are willing to take such courses in their first years on the job.[45]

The second and third recommendations called for making it harder for teachers to get tenure and to provide bonuses for highly effective teachers in schools serving low-income students.

What would prove to be the most controversial of the proposals, putting Democrats in conflict with the teachers' unions, was the fourth recommendation for evaluating teachers based on how much an individual teacher raised class test scores. The report did not call for abandoning traditional measures, such as observations and principal evaluations, but called for "some measure of 'value-added', or the average gain in performance for students assigned to each teacher."[46] One of the authors of the report, Harvard Professor Thomas Kane, was a champion of using "value-added" methods for teacher evaluation. In the previously stated recommendation of bonuses for "effective" teachers in low-income schools, the word "effective" refers to raising student test scores.

Democrats for Education Reform supported the report's call for federal action in implementing a "value-added" method of judging teacher performance: "Recommendation 5: Provide federal grants to help states that link student performance with the effectiveness of individual teachers over time."[47]

Race to the Top and Democrats for Education Reform

In 2009, Democrats for Education Reform sent their recommendations to the U.S. Secretary of Education Arne Duncan. The recommendations were described as a "series of issue briefs in which Democrats for Education Reform will present innovative ideas for Education Secretary Arne Duncan's $5 billion 'Race to the Top' initiative."[48]

One brief sent to the Secretary of Education emphasized alternative routes to teacher certification.[49] Challenging traditional college teacher training programs and traditional certification, the Democrats for Education Reform brief, titled "Enhancing Entry Points To The Teaching Profession," championed alternative routes to teacher certification with the claim, "Studies have shown that teachers prepared through alternative preparation programs are just as effective in the classroom as teachers prepared through traditional programs."[50] Indirectly, this statement can be considered an attack of teacher education college faculty.

The brief's recommendations paralleled those of the Hamilton report:

What States Must Do
States can support the growth of high-quality alternative teacher certification programs by:

• funding state-level, high quality alternative certification programs that have these characteristics;

- ensuring that alternative teacher certification programs are affordable to a wide range of nontraditional candidates by strategically requiring university coursework and learning experiences that are essential to a beginning teacher;
- specifying the competencies new teachers must demonstrate in order to be certified, rather than the numbers of courses or credit hours new teachers should take. Providers of teacher preparation programs could then design courses and learning experiences to ensure that new teachers demonstrate these skills;
- selecting candidates for alternative teacher certification who have already demonstrated mastery of their content are and only need training in teaching methods.[51]

Fast track?

These ideas were incorporated in President Obama's competitive Race to the Top. For instance, a high score was given to states that provided alternative routes to both teacher and principal certification:

D. Great Teachers and Leaders (138 points)
State Reform Conditions Criteria
(D)(1) Providing high-quality pathways for aspiring teachers and principals (21 points)
The extent to which the State has—

(i) legal, statutory, or regulatory provisions that *allow alternative routes to certification (as defined in this notice) for teachers and principals*, particularly *routes that allow for providers in addition to institutions of higher education*;
(ii) alternative routes to certification (as defined in this notice) that are in use [author's emphasis].[52]

Also, the Race to the Top called for teacher training focused on performance in contrast to course credit for obtaining teacher certification. In addition, Race to the Top called for linking student test scores to the credentialing program of teachers and principals.

(D)(4) Improving the effectiveness of teacher and principal preparation programs
The extent to which the State has a high-quality plan and ambitious yet achievable annual targets to—

(i) link student achievement and student growth (both as defined in this notice) data to the students' teachers and principals, to link this information to the in-State programs where those teachers and principals were prepared for credentialing, and to publicly report the data for each credentialing program in the State.[53]

Democrats for Education Reform also recommended to U.S. Secretary of Education Arne Duncan in a brief titled, "A Great Teacher For Every Child," that student test scores or, in the words of the brief, "student performance," be used in teacher evaluations. This was referred to as data-driven reform.

Data-Driven Reform

- Student-level data is used to drive policies that measure classroom- and school-level teacher effectiveness to evaluate teacher performance and inform professional development.
- States that have erected a firewall between teachers and student performance for the purpose of evaluating teachers and informing tenure decisions, like New York and California, should be made to change their policies or be disqualified from receiving Race to the Top funds.
- Priority should be given to states that have in place, and are able and willing to utilize, a system that follows teacher performance and tracks teacher effectiveness from the time of completion of their postsecondary education and allows evaluation of both pre-service and in-service training.[54]

In the Race to the Top, these recommendations were incorporated as:

(D)(2) Improving teacher and principal effectiveness based on performance

(i) establish clear approaches to measuring student growth (as defined in this notice) and measure it for each individual student; *Student Learning Outcomes*

(ii) design and implement rigorous, transparent, and fair evaluation systems for teachers and principals that (a) differentiate effectiveness using multiple rating categories *that take into account data on student growth* as a significant factor, and (b) are designed and developed with teacher and principal involvement [author's emphasis].[55] *Standardized tests don't.*

Democrats for Education Reform continued advocating value-added measurements of teacher performance. These proposals were incorporated in a 2011 letter sent by the Democrats for Education Reform and other organizations, and posted on the Democrats for Education website, to the Senate Committee on Health, Education, Labor and Pensions and the House of Representatives' Education and Workforce Committee considering the reauthorization of the ESEA. The letter proposed:

NEW TEACHER EVALUATION SYSTEMS

- All states and districts should begin moving immediately to create teacher evaluation systems comprised of multiple measures that are part of a single statewide assessment of teacher effectiveness. Criteria should include, at a minimum:

o   a state-determined method for *measuring teacher impact on student growth in tested academic subjects and grades, as a predominant factor in a teacher's evaluation* [author's emphasis].[56]

Charter Schools and Poverty

Democrats for Education Reform recommended expansion of charter schools as part of the Race to the Top.[57] In the past, charter schools were promoted as giving all parents more educational choices. In the Obama administration, charter schools are thought of as primarily meeting the needs of "disadvantaged" students. In this context, charter schools became part of a new War on Poverty. For instance, Lisa Macfarlane, Democrats for Education Reform Washington State Director, defended charter schools in Washington State with an emphasis on them serving disadvantaged students: "Our country's top Democrat, Barack Obama, the man we all fought to elect, is a big charter school fan. He believes in the ability of *successful charter schools to help some of our most educationally disadvantaged kids* [author's emphasis]."[58] She provided the following reasons for supporting charter schools:

- High quality public charter schools are successfully closing achievement gaps.
- High quality public charter schools can give underserved parents a choice and voice in their education.[59]

The Democrats for Education Reform's brief, "Public Charter Schools And High-Quality Pre-K," linked charter schools to Pre-K education. Pre-K education, similar to the Democratic supported Head Start program, is presented as a solution to the education of children from low-income families. Both charter schools and Pre-K education were to be part of a new War on Poverty. The brief asserts:

Research shows that between one-third and one-half of the achievement gap already exists by the time children begin first grade. Children from low-income families receive less support for early language, literacy, cognitive and social-emotional development than their more affluent peers. By age three, the typical disadvantaged child has heard 30 million fewer words than children from affluent families. Low-income children are also less likely to be read to and watch more TV than their middle-class and affluent peers. Low-income families are often under increased economic and other stresses that can also negatively affect children's development.[60]

The brief proposed:

> States should enact policies to encourage the creation of Pre-K Charter Schools to deliver high-quality early education to 3- and 4-year-olds. At a time when state budget woes threaten many Pre-K investments, this approach would enable states to use stimulus funds to expand children's access to high-quality early education programs, while maintaining a diverse, publicly accountable network of Pre-K providers.[61]

Its recommendations are to:

1. ensure that the state's charter school law explicitly authorizes charter schools to offer Pre-K programs;
2. amend the state charter school law and/or the state school funding formula law to allow public charter schools that serve 3- and 4-year-olds to receive per pupil funds for these students through the state's school funding formula;
3. exempt Pre-K charters from state caps on the number of charter schools that may be opened. This allows states to use Pre-K chartering to expand access to quality early education without bumping up against state charter school caps.[62]

The recommendations of Democrats for Education Reform that Pre-K education and charter schools be targeted for "disadvantaged" students (the terms used to describe this set of students varies and in the Race to the Top they are described as "high-need") were included in the Race to the Top:

> The Secretary is particularly interested in applications that include practices, strategies, or programs to improve educational outcomes for *high-need students* who are young children (pre-kindergarten through third grade) by enhancing the quality of preschool programs. Of particular interest are proposals that support practices that (i) improve school readiness (including social, emotional, and cognitive); and (ii) improve the transition between preschool and kindergarten [author's emphasis].[63]

The Race to the Top gave 40 points for: "Ensuring successful conditions for high-performing charters and other innovative schools (40 points)." Similar to the Democrats for Education Reform, Race to the Top provided incentives to ensure that States adjust their caps on the number of charter schools to ensure growth. In the words of Race to the Top, a State's "charter school law . . . [should] not prohibit or effectively inhibit increasing the number of high-performing charter schools."[64]

Democrats and Common Curriculum Standards

Since the 1980s, there has been a call from both major political parties' supported national curriculum standards. It is important to note that curriculum standards means *standardization* of the curriculum. The emphasis on standardization is important because early arguments for a standardized curriculum wanted to ensure that low-income students received the same quality of education as other students. The complaint was that those in schools serving low-income students were receiving a dumbed-down curriculum as compared to their counterparts in schools serving high-income students. In addition, it was asserted, standards were needed to prepare students for competition in a global labor market. In summary, there have been two arguments for common core standards with one argument emphasizing equality of educational opportunity for all students and the other focused on improving the U.S. economy.

On April 18, 1991, President George H. W. Bush unveiled Goals 2000—plans for achieving national education goals by the year 2000. Goals 2000 called for creating voluntary "American Achievement Tests" for grades 4, 8, and 12. The tests would cover five core subjects and students would be measured by "world-class standards." To accomplish this goal, the Bush administration, in cooperation with Congress and the National Governors Association, created the National Council on Education Standards and Testing (NCEST). The National Governors Association would continue to play an important role in creating national standards with the issuance in 2010 of the Common Core State Curriculum Standards.[65]

As Governor of Arkansas and prior to being President, Bill Clinton was elected in 1986 as vice chairperson of the National Governors Association. The chairperson of the organization was Lamar Alexander of Tennessee. It was in 1989 that Republican President H. W. Bush asked the National Governors Association to develop his plans for implementing Goals 2000. Referring to Bush's Goals 2000, Clinton gave this reminder to readers of his 1996 campaign book: "In 1989, I and the rest of the nation's governors ... were convinced that the more you expect of students, the more they expect of themselves and more they achieve."[66] World-class standards and tests, according to this argument, would help to achieve equality of educational opportunity and increase student achievement and help American workers compete in the global labor market. These principles would be shared by Republicans and Democrats, which would lead to their bipartisan support of No Child Left Behind.

In the 1990s, the Democrats stressed the importance of curriculum standards for providing equality of educational opportunity; those in schools serving low-income students would be taught the same things as schools serving high-income students. Fueling the concern about equality of educational opportunity was the 1991 publication of Jonathan Kozol's *Savage Inequalities: Children in America's Schools*.[67] Kozol painted a bleak picture of the differences between rich and poor public schools. Ensconced in protected suburbs, the rich and almost rich, according to Kozol, could provide their children with public schools filled with small classes, up-to-date educational materials, the best teachers, and an easy path to college. In contrast, the poor, often represented in the book as racial minorities, attended schools with deteriorating buildings, classes with too many students, outdated educational materials, and poor teachers. Writing in *Time* magazine, Emily Mitchell commented, "Kozol has written a searing exposé of the extremes of wealth and poverty in America's school system and the blighting effect on poor children."[68]

Standards and accountability were part of the legislation signed by Clinton in 1994 called the Goals 2000: Educate America Act and the School-to-Work Act. Unlike the later No Child Left Behind legislation, the academic standards proposed in this legislation were to be voluntary. In supporting the Goals 2000: Educate America Act, Democrats accepted the unproven assumption that increasing educational standards and making schools accountable would improve the schooling of American workers, and consequently lead to increased wages and decreased economic inequalities. Two months after the signing of the legislation, Marshall Smith, Clinton's undersecretary of education, speaking at a Brookings Institute conference on national standards asserted:

> The need for American students to learn more demanding content and skills became increasingly clear in the 1980s. The United States faces great challenges: internally, by the need to maintain a strong democracy in a complex and diverse society; externally, by a competitive economic environment that will be dominated by high-skills jobs.[69]

Marshall repeated an unquestioned assumption of the standards movement that children will learn more if they are challenged by more difficult standards. Concerning Clinton's Goals 2000 legislation, Marshall contended that high academic standards will result in high academic achievement for all students because "it builds on our understanding that all children can learn to higher levels than we have previously thought."[70]

The Democratic strategy assumed that under the new standards all students would have equal access to the teachers, books, educational materials, and laboratories required to meet national or state academic standards. Goals 2000: Educate America Act and Improving America's Schools Act represented an important change in the Democrats' traditional concern with equality of educational opportunity. The emphasis was no longer on desegregation and compensatory education programs. Now the focus was on uniformity through application of the same standards and accountability to all U.S. children. In this context, equality of educational opportunity meant equality of curricula, or in other words, every student would have an equal chance to learn a uniform state curriculum.

The Goals 2000: Educate America Act was also to overcome "savage inequalities" in the American school system. The legislation introduced opportunity-to-learn (OTL) standards as "the criteria for ... assessing ... [the ability] of the education system ... to provide all students with an opportunity to learn the material in voluntary national content standards or state content standards."[71] This meant that educational and other experts would have to find "scientific" measurements of school inequalities. The OTL standards held out the hope of finally addressing the issue of inequalities in educational opportunity. In the past, Republicans and Democrats skillfully avoided the politically charged issue of equal funding of school systems. Upper- and middle-class suburbanites were unwilling to give up their educational advantages, and they resisted being taxed to upgrade poorer school districts.[72]

The OTL standards were to remedy the inequality problems posed by national and state tests. According to Andrew Porter of the Wisconsin Center for Education Research, one of the federal government's experts hired to make scientific sense of the standards, "The initial motivation for OTL standards stems from an equity concern that high-stakes assessments of student achievement are fair only if students have had an adequate opportunity to learn the content assessed in those high-stakes tests."[73] The OTL recommendations reflect concerns raised in Kozol's *Savage Inequalities*. For instance, how can there be equal preparation for high stakes tests if some students attend overcrowded and deteriorating classrooms and they do not have access to required academic courses? How can students be adequately prepared for testing if their teachers are not prepared and do not have professional environments in which to work? The following is a list of some OTL recommendations targeting learning environments, curricula, and quality teachers.

- Schools should have enough physical space to accommodate all their students safely.
- Schools should have an adequate number of teachers and classrooms to ensure optimum class size.
- Students should have access to textbooks and educational facilities.
- Teachers should have the materials, time, private space, and support staff they need for lesson preparation and professional development.
- All students should have access to high level courses that will allow them to meet performance and content standards and provide them with good career opportunities.[74]

The OTL standards did not gain support in the 1994 Congress. This left Democrat Bill Clinton with a serious flaw in efforts to create a voluntary standards and accountability program. How could students attending poorly equipped schools with limited curricula and low-quality teachers be adequately prepared? The only hope was to rely on preschool programs like Head Start and compensatory education programs reauthorized in the Improving America's Schools Act. But these programs could do little to overcome the "savage inequalities" that could easily result in inequality in test results. Consequently, the Democratic education agenda in the 1996 campaign stressed academic standards without discussing OTL standards. The 1996 Democratic platform detailed the Party's general concept of standards: "We must hold students, teachers, and schools to the highest standards. Every child should be able to read by the end of the third grade. Students should be required to demonstrate competency and achievement for promotion or graduation."[75]

Increased funding of Head Start was the major claim Democrats could make towards preparing all students for academic standards and accountability. The 1996 Democratic platform summarized the Clinton administration's educational successes: "We passed Goals 2000 to help schools set high standards, and find the resources they need to succeed: the best books, the brightest teachers, the most up-to-date technology."[76] It should be noted that the platform refers to helping schools to "find" the best books, teachers, and technology rather than funding to pay for them.

In Clinton's last inaugural address he limited the comments on education to a panegyric to educational standards and the knowledge required by the global economy. There was no mention of OTL standards that would ensure equality of educational opportunity in meeting the standards outlined in Goals 2000. Clinton said:

> Our schools will have the highest standards in the world, igniting the spark of possibility in the eyes of every girl and every boy. And the doors of higher education will be open to all. The knowledge and power of the information age will be within reach not just of the few but of every classroom, every library, every child. Parents and children will have time not only to work but to read and play together. And the plans they make at their kitchen table will be those of a better home, a better job, the certain chance to go to college.[77]

After the 2000 election of President George W. Bush, Democrats were quick to accuse President Bush of stealing their ideas after the passage in 2001 of No Child Left Behind. The accusation was based on President Clinton's championship of standards and accountability and Democratic candidate Al Gore's reiteration of the Democratic vision of the standards movement during his failed 2000 Democratic campaign. During the 2000 campaign, Gore published an education agenda containing the familiar theme that school standards were necessary for global competition. The Gore agenda asserted that he would "build on and extend the aggressive efforts since 1993 to improve our schools through higher standards, extra help to students who need it the most, and equal access to higher education."[78]

Title I of the No Child Left Behind Act contained the provisions for creating curriculum standards and accountability through standardized testing—remember that the legislation was a reauthorization of the 1965 Elementary and Secondary Education Act in which Title I focused on compensatory programs for low-income families. An important difference was that the 1965 Title I targeted a particular group of students whereas in No Child Left Behind all students were included. In other words, equality of educational opportunity was to be achieved in this new form of Title I by teaching a standardized curriculum to all students and holding all schools accountable through standardized testing of all students. Schools failing to make adequate progress in improving test scores were to be closed and restructured. Restructuring failing schools was to help provide equality of educational opportunity. Those provisions of No Child Left Behind that addressed the standards and accountability were in Title I, "Improving the Academic Achievement of the Disadvantaged," which required states to create academic standards aligned with state tests. If a school that received federal Title I funding failed to achieve adequate yearly progress two years in a row, it would be provided with technical assistance and its students would be offered a choice of other public schools to attend. Students in schools failing to make adequate progress three years in a row were required to offer supplemental educational services, including private tutoring. A school that continued to fail would be subjected to outside corrective measures, including being restructured.[79] The 2004 Democratic presidential candidate John Kerry supported No Child Left Behind. In the Democratic campaign book, *Our Plan for America: Stronger At Home, Respected in the World*, Kerry highlighted that he voted for the legislation.[80] So by the 2008 election, Democrats were committed to state development of academic standards.

In summary, since the 1990s Democrats were committed to supporting academic standards to provide equality of educational opportunities and to enhance America's ability to compete in the global economy. Along the way, Democrats abandoned OTL standards in favor of closing and/or restructuring failing schools to achieve equality of educational opportunity. Was the reason the financial costs of ensuring schools were equal under OTL standards? Or did the application of common standards ensure that students in schools serving primarily low-income students would have the same educational opportunities as schools serving middle- and upper-income students? Certainly, economic and racial integration of state school systems was never considered, which might have threatened wealthy public school districts. Under No Child Left Behind, wealthy suburban school districts could feel safe that their privileges were protected.

Common Core State Standards: Democrats for Education Reform and Race to the Top

Democrats for Education Reform's brief, "World Class Standards And Assessments," urged President Obama to include in the Race to the Top common core standards, which they stated, "must be part of a seamless, integrated state system of P-16 education."[81] The Democrats for Education Reform linked common core standards directly to the needs of the global economy: "It is widely agreed that the U.S. should raise academic standards, in-line with global economic demands for a college-educated, high-tech workforce."[82] The Obama administration was warned to avoid past errors in trying to create national curriculum standards, including ensuring companies producing tests aligned them with national standards: "This time around, the federal government must ensure that states and the major testing companies break the patterns that have rendered mediocre and unimaginative assessment products in the past."[83] This issue will be discussed later when we consider the profits gained by companies with the implementation of Common Core State Standards, particularly the testing and textbook giant Pearson.

The Race to the Top rejected the idea of P-16 standards and limited them to P-12. It is not clear what will happen if curriculum standards are imposed on colleges.[84] The Race to the Top called for: "Adopting standards and assessments that prepare students to succeed in college and the workplace and to compete in the global economy."[85]

Preparing students for the global economy was the major goal of the Common Core State Standards released by the National Governors Association in 2010. As officially stated, the Common Core State Standards were to prepare students to enter a global workforce:

> The Common Core State Standards provide a consistent, clear understanding of what students are expected to learn, so teachers and parents know what they need to do to help them. The standards are designed to be robust and relevant to the real world, *reflecting the knowledge and skills that our young people need for success in college and careers. With American students fully prepared for the future, our communities will be best positioned to compete successfully in the global economy* [author's emphasis].[86]

There is no reference in the Common Core State Standards to the type of proposals made by President Clinton's Opportunity to Learn Standards. In other words, the Common Core State Standards did not address the issue of providing same quality of schooling for all students to learn the Standards.

It is stated in the Common Core State Standards Initiative that a standardized curriculum will provide an equal education because all students will be taught the same things. In responding to the question, "Why is the Common Core State Standards Initiative important?", the official response was:

> High standards that are consistent across states provide teachers, parents, and students with a set of clear expectations that are aligned to the expectations in college and careers. *The standards promote equity by ensuring all students, no matter where they live, are well prepared* with the skills and

knowledge necessary to collaborate and compete with their peers in the
United States and abroad [author's emphasis].[87]

As stated throughout the Common Core State Standards, the primary goal
is to prepare students for work or college with the assumption that college will
be a career training institution. There is no statement in the goals about transmit-
ting American or global culture to students or preparing students for a life
of happiness and enjoyable use of leisure time. The Standards are all about
preparation for work.

By July 2012, all but four states adopted the Standards. The Common
Core State Standards affect teacher training and testing. Many teacher education
programs include, particularly in courses on methods of instruction and curriculum, the Common Core State Standards. Also, national and state tests used in
public schools are to be aligned with the requirements of the Common Core
State Standards.

Preparation for work or college is tied to a larger goal of improving the
ability of the U.S. to compete in a global economic system. An example of
both the political nature of the Common Core State Standards and its links to
concerns about global economic competition is the statement made by Georgia's
Governor Sonny Perdue in approving the work of the National Governors
Association:

> American competitiveness relies on an education system that can adequately
> prepare our youth for college and the workforce. When American students
> have the skills and knowledge needed in today's jobs, our communities will
> be positioned to compete successfully in the global economy.[88]

As officially explained by the Common Core State Standards Initiative,
"Preparing America's Students for College & Career":

> These standards define the knowledge and skills students should have
> within their K-12 education careers so that they will graduate high school
> able to succeed in entry-level, credit-bearing academic college courses and
> in workforce training programs. The standards:
>
> - are aligned with college and work expectations;
> - are clear, understandable and consistent;
> - include rigorous content and application of knowledge through high-
>   order skills;
> - build upon strengths and lessons of current state standards;
> - are informed by other top performing countries, so that all students are
>   prepared to succeed in our global economy and society; and
> - are evidence-based.[89]

Despite the claim that the Common Score State Standards are "evidenced-based," there is no existing research supporting the claim that the Standards will lead to students being more competitive in the global workforce. This would require longitudinal research showing that over a number of years the Standards actually contributed to enhancing the ability of the U.S. economy within the global economy. In fact, it might be impossible to measure, given the variety of influences on the economy, whether or not the Standards actually make students and the nation more competitive in the global workforce and economy.

By focusing on preparation for work, the Common Core State Standards limit the range of student education as exemplified in the area of literacy instruction. Common Core State Standards call for increasing the reading of nonfiction and decreasing the reading of fiction. Eliminated from the Standards are goals of relating student feelings to a reading selection or in writing about their feelings. The goal is learning to read and write for work or a college course.

David Coleman, an architect of the Common Core State Standards and President of the College Board, explained his push for students to write fewer personal and opinion pieces. As reported by Tamar Lewin, he asserted that in the working world a person would not say: "Johnson, I need a market analysis by Friday, but before that I need a compelling account of your childhood."[90]

As reported by Catherine Gewertz, David Liben, a former New York City teacher and now a senior literacy specialist with Student Achievement Partners, told the teachers that the Common Core State Standards "virtually eliminate[s] text-to-self connections." Liben directed teachers to eliminate from basal readers any questions dealing with how students feel about a reading along with any questions asking about the meaning of the reading in the students' life. "In college and careers, no one cares how you feel," Liben said; "Imagine being asked to write a memo on why your company's stock price has plummeted: 'Analyze why and tell me how you feel about it'."[91]

As I will discuss in the next chapter, the mandated readings in the Common Core State Standards reflects a limiting multicultural literature and a stress on American and Anglo-American culture. The Standards for Reading state:

> The standards mandate certain critical types of content for all students, including classic myths and stories from around the world, foundational U.S. documents, seminal works of American literature, and the writings of Shakespeare. The standards appropriately defer the many remaining decisions about what and how to teach to states, districts, and schools.[92]

The multicultural debates of the 20th century were resolved in the Common Core State Standards with the only mandated global literature being "myths and stories from around the world." An emphasis on schools promoting nationalism is reflected in the mandate for using "foundational U.S. documents, seminal works of American literature." The mandating of the writings of Shakespeare is one of the peculiar parts of the Common Core State Standards. Why Shakespeare rather than other great global writers? Is it because it reflects Anglo-Saxon traditions so greatly prized by American conservatives? Or is Shakespeare included because he is a favorite of English teachers? Certainly, there is no research that proves reading Shakespeare enhances a student's ability to compete in the global workforce. This issue, as I discuss in Chapter 2, goes to the heart of the political debate about multiculturalism.

The strange appearance of Shakespeare and American nationalism in the Standards, without any proof that they enhance global competitiveness, and the lack of long-range research evidence that the Standards enhance the ability to compete in a global workforce, suggests that the Standards might be primarily based on political and cultural decisions.

Conclusion

The lack of longitudinal research proving the current Democratic agenda will actually improve the ability of the U.S. to compete in the global economy or provide educational equality suggests other motivations for these educational changes. The Democratic agenda, as articulated by the Democrats for Education Reform and contained in the Race to the Top, reflects certain political perspectives on economic improvement, equality of educational opportunity, culture, language, and teachers. Also, there is a language issue with the use of the word "reform." The word "reform" connotes improvement in contrast to using the more neutral word "change." However, when we consider the often stated goal of changing schools to improve America's ability to compete in the global economy, there is no research showing that common core standards and accompanying tests, charter schools, changes in credentialing and evaluation of teachers or preschool will make the U.S. more competitive in the global economy.

Without supporting research it is important to examine the motives, assumptions, and political connections of the proponents of this agenda. In fact, as I have suggested throughout this chapter, it might be impossible to design a research study that shows that these education changes actually improved America's ability to compete in global markets because of the many other causal economic factors involved. Even if a research study could be designed it would not be completed until the children affected by this reform agenda go through a full cycle of schooling from preschool to high school graduation. Selecting 2016 as an arbitrary date, though it is doubtful all changes will be in place by this date, we would be looking at four-year-olds entering preschool in 2016 and graduating possibly in 2030. Measuring the effect of the 2030 high school graduate on the economy would require examining economic changes after these graduates are in the labor market. How long does it take for a high school graduate to affect the economy? Can conclusions be made about the effect on the economy ten years after high school graduation? Twenty years? In other words, at a bare minimum, we would not know the results until 2030 or later.

Will the current Democratic education agenda result in equality of educational opportunity? The assumption is that equality of educational opportunity will be achieved if all students are exposed to the same common core standards and assessments; to teachers who have undergone new credentialing and evaluation methods; to preschool; and to the opportunity to attend charter schools. Again, there is problem of longitudinal research studies. What we do know is that the current Democratic agenda avoids any suggestion of economic or racial integration of schools or integrating rich and poor school districts. In fact, the issue of financial equality between public school districts is not even suggested in the reform plans.

Given the lack of longitudinal research it is important to examine why the current Democratic agenda was proposed. I will do this in Chapter 2 along with examining the cultural assumptions underlying the Common Core State Standards or, as it was called in the 20th century, the culture wars.

Notes

1 Democrats for Education Reform, "Statement of Principles." Retrieved from http://www.dfer.org/petition/SOP/ on February 12, 2013.
2 Steven Brill, *Class Warfare: Inside the Fight to Fix America's Schools* (New York: Simon & Schuster, 2012), pp. 219–226.
3 Public Prep, "Mission and Model." Retrieved from http://publicprep.org/about/mission on February 12, 2013.
4 Brill, *Class Warfare*, p. 132.
5 U.S. Department of Education, "Race to the Top Program: Executive Summary" (November 2009), pp. 7, 9, 11. Retrieved from http://www2.ed.gov/programs/racetothetop/executive-summary.pdf on January 23, 2013.
6 Arne Duncan, "The Race To The Top Begins: Remarks By Secretary" (July 24, 2009). Retrieved from http://www.ed.gov/news/speeches/race-top-begins on January 10, 2013.
7 "A World Class Education for Every Child," *Renewing America's Promise 2008 Democratic National Platform*, p. 33. Retrieved from http://www.presidency.ucsb.edu/ws/index.php?pid=78283 on February 20, 2013.
8 "An Economy that Out-Educates the World and Offers Greater Access to Higher Education and Technical Training," *Moving America Forward 2012 Democratic National Platform*, p. 6. Retrieved from http://assets.dstatic.org/dnc-platform/2012-National-Platform.pdf on December 2, 2012.
9 Common Core State Standards Initiative, "Mission Statement." Retrieved from http://www.corestandards.org/ on January 13, 2013.
10 Catherine Rampell, "It Takes a B.A. to Find a Job as a File Clerk," *The New York Times* (February 19, 2013). Retrieved from http://www.nytimes.com/2013/02/20/business/college-degree-required-by-increasing-number-of-companies.html?ref=todayspaper&_r=0&pagewanted=print on February 20, 2013.
11 Keith Bradsher, "In China, Families Bet It All on College for Their Children," *The New York Times* (February 16, 2013). Retrieved from http://www.nytimes.com/2013/02/17/business/in-china-families-bet-it-all-on-a-child-in-college.html?pagewanted=all on February 20, 2013.

12 Public Law 107–110—January 8, 2002, No Child Left Behind Act of 2001. Retrieved from the U.S. Department of Education, http://www.ed.gov/policy/elsec/leg/esea02/107-110.pdf on February 1, 2009.

13 Democratic Party Platform of 1992, *A New Covenant with the American People* (July 13, 1992), p. 5. Retrieved from the American Presidency Project Document Archive http://www.presidency.ucsb.edu/ws/index. php?pid=pid29610 on January 5, 2009.

14 "Elementary and Secondary Education Act of 1965, Public Law 89–110," reprinted in Stephen Bailey and Edith Mosher, *ESEA: The Office of Education Administers a Law* (Syracuse, NY: Syracuse University Press, 1968), pp. 235–266.

15 Public Law 107–110, 107th Congress, January 8, 2002 [H.R. 1], "No Child Left Behind Act of 2001" (Washington, DC: U.S. Government Printing Office, 2002), p. 1.

16 Lyndon B. Johnson, "The State of the Union Message to Congress, 8 January 1964," in *A Time for Action: A Selection from the Speeches and Writings of Lyndon B. Johnson* (New York: Atheneum, 1964), pp. 164–179.

17 U.S. Congress, House Committee on Education and Labor, *Aid to Elementary and Secondary Education: Hearings before the General Subcommittee on Education of the Committee on Education and Labor*, 89th Cong., 1st sess., 1965 (Washington, DC: U.S. Government Printing Office, 1965), pp. 63–82.

18 "The Problem of Poverty in America," in *The Annual Report of the Council of Economic Advisers* (Washington, DC: U.S. Government Printing Office, 1964).

19 Ibid.

20 Ibid.

21 See Brian Keeley, *Human Capital: How What You Know Shapes Your Life* (Paris: OECD, 2007), pp. 28–35; and Phillip Brown and Hugh Lauder, "Globalization, Knowledge and the Myth of the Magnet Economy," in *Education, Globalization and Social Change*, edited by Hugh Lauder, Phillip Brown, Jo-Anne Dillabough, and A. H. Halsey (Oxford: Oxford University Press, 2006), pp. 317–340.

22 Quoted in Keeley, *Human Capital*, p. 29.

23 Gary Becker, "The Age of Human Capital," in *Education, Globalization and Social Change*, edited by Hugh Lauder, Phillip Brown, Jo-Anne Dillabough, and A. H. Halsey (Oxford: Oxford University Press, 2006), p. 292.

24 Gary Becker, *Human Capital* (New York: Columbia University Press, 1964).

25 Quoted in Joel Spring, *The American School: From Puritans to No Child Left Behind*, 7th ed. (New York: McGraw-Hill, 2008), p. 407.

26 Ibid.

27 Democratic Party Platform of 1968, *The Terms of Our Duty* (August 28, 1968), p. 42. Retrieved from the American Presidency Project Document Archive http://www.presidency.ucsb.edu/ws/index.php?pid=29604 on January 14, 2009.

28 Democratic Party Platform of 1972, *New Directions* (July 10, 1972), p. 19. Retrieved from the American Presidency Project Document Archive http://www.presidency.ucsb.edu/ws/index.php?pid=29605 on January 14, 2009.

29 Democratic Party Platform of 1996, *Today's Democratic Party: Meeting America's Challenges, Protecting America's Values* (August 26, 1996), p. 5. Retrieved from the American Presidency Project Document Archive http://www.presidency.ucsb.edu/ws/index.php?pid=29612 on January 8, 2009.

30 Democratic Party Platform of 2000, *Prosperity, Progress, and Peace*, p. 9. Retrieved from the American Presidency Project Document Archive http://www.presidency.ucsb.edu/ws/index.php?pid=29612 on January 5, 2009.

31 2008 Democratic Party Platform, "RENEWING AMERICA'S PROMISE." Retrieved from http://www.presidency.ucsb.edu/ws/index.php?pid=78283 on February 22, 2013.

32 Barack Obama, *2013 State of the Union Address*. Retrieved from http://www.whitehouse.gov/state-of-the-union-2013#webform_on February 21, 2013.

33 Democrats for Education Reform, "Statement of Principles." Retrieved from http://www.dfer.org/petition/SOP/ on February 20, 2013.

34 Democrats for Education Reform, "Statement of Principles on Teacher Quality and Effectiveness in the Reauthorization of the Elementary and Secondary Education Act" (October 7, 2011). Retrieved from http://www.dfer.org/ESEA%20Priorities%20Teacher%20Quality.Coalition%20Letter.Final.pdf on February 20, 2013.

35 Democrats for Education Reform, "What We Stand For." Retrieved from http://www.dfer.org/about/standfor/ on February 20, 2013.

36 Ibid.

37 Ibid.

38 Democrats for Education Reform, "Statement of Principles."

39 Rod Paige, *The War Against Hope: How Teachers' Unions Hurt Children, Hinder Teachers, and Endanger Public Education* (Nashville, TN: Thomas Nelson, 2006), p. 2.

40 Eileen White, "N.E.A. Steps Up Anti-Reagan Lobbying Effort" *Education Week* (January 12, 1982). Retrieved from http://www.edweek.org on February 26, 2009.

41 Ibid.

42 Paige, *The War Against Hope*.

43 Robert Gordon, Thomas J. Kane, and Douglas Staiger, *Identifying Effective Teachers Using Performance on the Job* (Washington, DC: The Brookings Institution, 2006).

44 Ibid., p. 7.

45 Ibid., p. 6.

46 Ibid., p. 6.

47 Ibid., p. 6.

48 Democrats for Education Reform, "Racing To The Top: American Recovery and Reinvestment Act Issues Brief Series #6: A Great Teacher For Every Child" (June 17, 2009), p. 2. Retrieved from http://www.dfer.org/top6/Race_to_Top_6.pdf on February 21, 2013.

49 Democrats for Education Reform, "Racing To The Top: American Recovery and Reinvestment Act Issues Brief Series #3: Enhancing Entry Points To The Teaching Profession" (June 17, 2009). Retrieved from http://www.dfer.org/Top3/Race_to_Top_3.pdf on February 21, 2013.

50 Ibid., p. 3.

51 Ibid., pp. 4–5.

52 U.S. Department of Education, "Race to the Top Program: Executive Summary," p. 9.

53 Ibid., p. 10.

54 Democrats for Education Reform, "Racing To The Top: American Recovery and Reinvestment Act Issues Brief Series #6: A Great Teacher For Every Child," p. 3.

55 U.S. Department of Education, "Race to the Top Program: Executive Summary," p. 9.

56 Democrats for Education Reform, "Statement of Principles on Teacher Quality and Effectiveness in the Reauthorization of the Elementary and Secondary Education Act."

57 Democrats for Education Reform, "Racing To The Top: American Recovery and Reinvestment Act Issues Brief Series#1: Public Charter Schools And High-Quality Pre-K" (June 17, 2009). Retrieved from http://www.dfer.org/Top1/Race_to_the_Top_1.pdf on February 21, 2013.

58 Lisa Macfarlane, "Why Democrats Support Charter Schools." Retrieved from http://www.dfer.org/2012/01/why_democrats_s.php on February 21, 2013.

59 Ibid.

60 Democrats for Education Reform, "Racing To The Top: American Recovery and Reinvestment Act Issues Brief Series#1: Public Charter Schools And High-Quality Pre-K," p. 4.

61 Ibid., p. 4.

62 Ibid., pp. 6–7.

63 U.S. Department of Education, "Race to the Top Program: Executive Summary," p. 4.

64 Ibid., p.11.

65 To examine the current Common Core State Standards created by the National Governors Association go to http://www.corestandards.org/.

66 Bill Clinton, *Between Hope and History: Meeting America's Challenges for the 21st Century* (New York: Times Books, 1996), p. 42.

67 Jonathan Kozol, *Savage Inequalities: Children in America's Schools* (New York: Crown, 1991).

68 Ibid., back cover of book.

69 Marshall S. Smith, "Education Reform in America's Public Schools: The Clinton Agenda," in *Debating the Future of American Education: Do We Need National Standards and Assessments?* edited by Diane Ravitch (Washington, DC: Brookings Institution, 1995), p. 9.

70 Ibid., p. 10.

71 *Improving America's Schools Act of 1994*, Title I—Amendments to the Elementary and Secondary Education Act of 1965. Retrieved from http://www.ed. gov/legislation/ESEA/sec1001.html on February 3, 2009. The legislation is quoted by Andrew Porter, "The Uses and Misuses of Opportunity-to-Learn Standards," in *Debating the Future of American Education: Do We Need National Standards and Assessments?* edited by Diane Ravitch (Washington, DC: Brookings Institution, 1995), p. 41.

72 As an example of how long the attempt has been made in the courts to achieve equality of spending between school districts, check Richard Lehne's now-dated book, *The Quest for Justice: The Politics of School Finance Reform* (New York: Longman, 1978). Jonathan Kozol's *Savage Inequalities* reinforced the concern about financial inequalities between school districts.

73 Porter, "The Uses and Misuses of Opportunity-to-Learn Standards," p. 41.

74 Wendy Schwartz, "Opportunity to Learn Standards: Their Impact on Urban Students." ERIC Identifier: ED389816 (New York: ERIC Clearing-house on Urban Education, 1995). Retrieved from http://www.ericdigests.org/1996-3/urban.htm on February 3, 2009.

75 Democratic Party platform of 1996, *Today's Democratic Party: Meeting America's Challenges, Protecting America's Values* (August 26, 1996), p. 9. Retrieved from the American Presidency Project Document Archive http://www.presidency.ucsb. edu/ws/index.php?pid=29611 on January 5, 2009.

76 Ibid., p. 8.

77 William J. Clinton, "Inaugural Address" (January 20, 1997), p. 4. Retrieved from the American Presidency Project Document Archive http://www.presidency.ucsb. edu/ws/print.php?pid=54183 on February 3, 2009.

78 "The Gore Agenda: Revolutionizing American Education in the 21st Century." Retrieved from http://www.ontheissues.org/al_gore.htm on October 3, 2000.

79 Quoted in Spring, *The American School*, p. 407.

80 John Kerry and John Edwards, *Our Plan for America: Stronger at Home, Respected in the World* (New York: Public Affairs, 2004).

81 Democrats for Education Reform, "Racing To The Top: American Recovery and Reinvestment Act Issues Brief Series #4: World Class Standards And Assessments" (June 17, 2009), p. 4. Retrieved from http://www.dfer.org/Top4/Race_to_Top_4.pdf on February 21, 2013.

82 Ibid., p. 3.

83 Ibid., p. 5.

84 At the time I was writing this edition, my university, the City University of New York, was embroiled in a heated controversy over the imposition of standards for general education involving the faculty, the union and the university administration. Standards,

among other things, means standardization of courses. Should college courses by standardized? What happens to academic freedom with standardization?

85 U.S. Department of Education, "Race to the Top Program: Executive Summary," p. 2.

86 Common Core State Standards Initiative, "Mission Statement."

87 Common Core State Standards Initiative, "Frequently Asked Questions." Retrieved from http://www.corestandards.org/resources/frequently-asked-questions on March 4, 2013.

88 Sonny Perdue "National Governors Association and State Education Chiefs Launch Common State Academic Standards," Common Core Standards Initiative. Retrieved from http://www.corestandards.org/articles/8-national-governors-association-and-state-education-chiefs-launch-common-state-academic-standards on May 7, 2011.

89 Common Core State Standards Initiative, "About the Standards." Retrieved from http://www.corestandards.org/about-the-standards on January 5, 2013.

90 Tamar Lewin, "Backer of Common Core School Curriculum Is Chosen to Lead College Board," *The New York Times* (May 16, 2012). Retrieved from http://www.nytimes.com/2012/05/16/education/david-coleman-to-lead-college-board.html on March 4, 2013.

91 Catherine Gewertz, "Teachers Embedding Standards in Basal-Reader Questions," *Education Week* (May 9, 2012). Retrieved from http://www.edweek.org/ew/articles/2012/04/26/30basal.h31.html?qs=Gewertz on May 10, 2012.

92 Common Core State Standards Initiative, "Key Points in English Language Arts: Reading." Retrieved from http://www.corestandards.org/resources/key-points-in-english-language-arts on July 8, 2013.

2

THE POLITICAL COUP KNOWN AS RACE TO THE TOP

"... the truth is that the largest funders of the 'reform' movement are the opposite of disinterested altruists. They are cutthroat businesspeople making shrewd financial investments in a movement that is less about educating children than about helping 'reform' funders hit pay dirt."[1]

What are the motives for backing Race to the Top, since it is not supported by longitudinal research findings? As I argue in this chapter, there are a variety of motives. Major factors are the ideological beliefs of the supporters, who are anti-union, including anti-teachers' unions, and believe that the traditional public school system is at fault for the growing inequality of income and the problems the U.S. faces in the global economy. Some of these same supporters resist the economic and racial integration of state school districts and appear to want to protect their educational advantages. Some investment firms and for-profit education industries back Race to the Top because its agenda promises increased earnings. Some have a faith in the ability of data, meaning student test scores and details of their social backgrounds, to improve the quality of teachers, end inequality of educational opportunity, and improve America's ability to compete in global markets. The belief in databases as a panacea for education is reflected in the comment by Frank Catalano of Intrinsic Strategy, a consulting firm focused on education and technology, that, "The hype in the tech press is that education is an engineering problem that can be fixed by technology."[2]

I will begin discussing the many motives behind Race to the Top by examining the interests of investment bankers and for-profit education companies. Then I will examine the lack of public school experience and the ideologies for the early supporters, particularly U.S. Secretary of Education Arne Duncan and the Democrats for Education Reform. Networks link all of the above—investment bankers, for-profit education companies, and reformers.

Investing in Race to the Top

The Education Industries Association (EIA), the lobbying group for for-profit education companies, distributed two papers, among many, calling for greater investment in the education sector. One is written for the American Enterprise Institute (AEI), an organization dedicated to promoting free market economics. It is called an "AEI Future of American Education Project" and titled "Private Capital and Public Education: Toward Quality At Scale"[3] The essay is written by Tom Vander Ark, who is a managing partner of the investment firm Learn Capital and, prior to that, Executive Director of Education for the ubiquitous Bill and Melinda Gates Foundation, which has been a major funder of many of the parts of the Race to the Top.[4] The investment portfolio of Learn Capital lists 28 for-profit education companies.[5]

Ark's essay is accompanied by a foreword by Frederick M. Hess, Director of Education Policy Studies at AEI, stressing the role of for-profit companies in achieving the goals of Race to the Top. Hess asserts that schools will improve with "the importance of for-profit education companies that can attract venture capital and that are better equipped to sustain and grow through profits and private equity."[6]

Ark uses a similar argument that government spending has been wasted by being channeled through a rigid education bureaucracy. To bring about real change, he asserts, requires the involvement of for-profit education industries funded by venture capital. In his words:

> While the public delivery system is inflexible and bureaucratic and provides an inadequate impetus for performance and improvement, non-profit organizations have weak incentives and limited ability to aggregate capital for research and development or scaled impact. In contrast, for-profit enterprises may have greater ability to attract talent and capital, incentives to achieve scaled impact, and the ability to utilize multiple business strategies.[7]

In the context of the changes advocated in Race to the Top, Ark writes, "Private capital and for-profit enterprises will play a vital role in creating tools that increase learning, staffing, and facilities productivity."[8]

Besides justifying for-profit education industries with claims that public school bureaucracies are inflexible, investment groups warn about the power of teachers' unions and assert that school reform will solve the problem of increasing inequality of incomes. An example of this argument can be found in a long, 332-page, investment report distributed by the Education Industry

Association and published by GSV Capital with the title: *American Revolution 2.0: How Education Innovation is Going to Revitalize America and Transform the U.S. Economy.*[9] The lead author of the report is Michael Moe, co-founder of GSV Capital and its Chief Investment Officer. The company's website describes him:

> Michael is well known and regarded as one of the world's preeminent authorities on growth investing. *His insights are routinely solicited by everyone from CNBC to Barron's to Congress.* Recognized as one of the best and brightest investors on Wall Street, his honors include *Institutional Investor's* "All American" research team, *The Wall Street Journal's* "Best on the Street" award, and being named by *Business Week* as "one of the best stock pickers in the country" [author's emphasis].[10]

The basic argument of *American Revolution 2.0* is that improving schools depends on greater involvement of the for-profit education sector. This will result, it is stated, in the American economy being revitalized and income inequalities being reduced.

The report conveys a fear that inequality of income will lead to some form of revolution—a revolution that they claim can be countered by an "education" revolution. The report asserts, "Occupy Wall Street (OWS) and adjacent uprisings have powerfully demonstrated that a large and growing segment of American society doesn't believe that they are participating in the future … Aristotle observed, 'Inequality is the parent of revolution'."[11] In fact, the report actually lists major revolutions from the 1910 Mexican Revolution to 2010 Arab Spring and on the page listing the revolutions is a photo of an Occupy Wall Street protester holding a sign saying, "One day the poor will have nothing left to eat but the rich."[12]

Of course, being a capital investment firm, the report does not advocate redistribution of wealth: "Joe the Plumber is right in that redistribution of wealth is not a sustainable economic philosophy, nor is it an American one."[13] They argue that using the tax system to reduce income inequalities could result in spreading "the seeds of class chaos [which] could easily result in a Robin Hood State instead of addressing the real issue of preparing people to be productive in the world we are in."[14] The real revolution, the report suggests, should be against the public schools: "The revolution America needs today is not against an oppressive monarchy, but rather *against an education system that has equally oppressive effects* [author's emphasis]."[15]

Using the metaphors of war and revolution, the report calls for a "Second American Revolution" declaring that they have the "arms and technology to fight this war."[16] This revolution will be led by for-profit technology companies providing learning products to schools. The "battlefield" is described as the "Unions" and "Status Quo Forces" versus "Change Agents." Showing a photo of an 18th-century American revolutionary soldier, the status quo forces are given as:

1. Unions and beneficiaries of current system
2. Tenure
3. No choice, no competition
4. For-profits for the enemy
5. Transparency is avoided.[17]

Fighting against the status quo, the report presents what it calls the "Arms Dealers."[18] These "arms dealers" are the for-profit education companies which the report presents as investment opportunities. First on the list is Rupert Murdoch's News Corporation accompanied by the note: "Recently rebranded 'Amplify' educational services division partnering with AT&T to provide purpose-built tablets and develop other digital learning platforms for K–12 Classrooms."[19] Second on the investment list is a major player in the testing field, Pearson, which the report notes: "Recent acquisitions of Schoolnet and TutorVista dramatically expand digital instruction footprint ... Continued investments/partnerships with Knewton, Tabula Digita, Inkling, and Florida Virtual support growth in digital learning."[20] Knewton is a pioneer in applying analytics to large data sets. The other "arms dealers" are MacMillan, McGraw Hill, Cengage Learning, Houghton Mifflin Harcourt, Scholastic, Blackboard, Dell, Apple, and Microsoft.[21]

American Revolution 2.0 and the American Enterprise essay "Private Capital and Public Education: Toward Quality At Scale" both suggest a motive for investment companies to support the Race to the Top agenda. As I explain in the next section, there is money to be made selling products to fulfill the Race to the Top, such as analytic education platforms, software and services to help use the data for "value-added" teacher and principal evaluations, and providing services to help integrate the Common Core State Standards into local curricula. And, of course, for-profit charter school management companies benefit from support by Race to the Top for expansion of charter schools. Regarding profits to be earned from charter schools, the National Education Policy Center reported in 2012 that:

> The number of states in which for-profit EMOs operated was 33 in 2010–2011. The for-profit education management industry expanded into Alaska and Hawaii this past year for the first time. Only one Alaska and one Hawaii school were fully managed by a for-profit EMO during this period.[22]

In other words, investors can make money from every aspect of Race to the Top.

Race to the Top and Education Industry

As discussed in the previous section, some investment companies consider the Race to the Top an opportunity for profitmaking companies to expand their role in the education market. Race to the Top requires: "Building data systems that measure student growth and success, and inform teachers and principals about how they can improve instruction."[23] The creation of a national school database benefits for-profit education companies, particularly technology companies. In fact, the new national school database is designed to aid for-profit education companies.

Work on the database began in 2011 when the Council of Chief State School Officers organized the Shared Learning Collaborative for the stated purpose of "reducing the burden on state budgets by building this technology on behalf of states and making it available to them as shared services."[24] The Shared Learning Collaborative, with the aid of Rupert Murdoch's Amplify, created a common infrastructure for data integration and application for schools. The database was designed to support the Common Core State Standards:

> This open source technology is designed to support the implementation of the Common Core State Standards and allow states and districts to integrate student data that currently exists in different source systems and formats and make it available to content and applications from many providers.[25]

The Council of Chief State School Officers received support for the project from the Bill and Melinda Gates Foundation and the Carnegie Corporation of New York. As the world's richest foundation focusing on education in the U.S., the Bill and Melinda Gates Foundation is considered the shadow education government with many of its workers being shared with the U.S. Department of Education.[26] While the more cynical might consider the involvement of the Gates Foundation as somehow related to the sale of education products by Microsoft, a more benign view is that the Gates Foundation reflects the mindset of its founder, namely that data and technology are the solution to many of the world's problems, including education.

In 2011, when the Council of Chief State School Officers gave a contract to Wireless Generation, now a part of Rupert Murdoch's Amplify, to develop the initial data framework, Wireless Generation was listed on the Shared Learning Collaborative website as a supporting organization and partner.[27] The work of the Shared Learning Collaborative was eventually housed in the nonprofit company inBloom. As described on inBloom's website, the Shared Learning Collaborative: "custom-built all the inBloom software components and *has worked with education technology companies and developers to encourage the development of inBloom-compatible applications* [author's emphasis]."[28]

InBloom skirts a thin line between protecting the privacy of student data while offering it to for-profit companies. On the one hand, inBloom states as one of its guiding principles: "We recognize the sensitivity of storing student data and place the utmost importance on the privacy and security of that data."[29] On the other hand, inBloom states another guiding principle: "We ensure availability of and access to inBloom services by creating cost-effective technology services for states and districts of all sizes, and partnering with companies ranging from start-ups to established education technology leaders."[30] More specifically, inBloom describes its vision as: "Partners with education technology companies, content providers and developers to support the creation of products compatible with this infrastructure."[31] As envisioned by inBloom, for-profit technology companies will create applications that utilize the database to create personalized learning.[32]

InBloom's creation was announced at the same time that Murdoch's Amplify, which built inBloom's infrastructure, introduced its tablet at the March 4–7, 2013 SXSWedu Conference in Austin, Texas.[33] Reaping profit from the database, Amplify sponsored the SXSWedu Conference and was listed as:

> Amplify
> Amplify is a new organization dedicated to K-12 education by creating digital products and services that empower students, teachers and parents in new ways. Amplify will enhance the potential of students with new curricular experiences, support teachers with new instructional tools and engage parents through extended learning opportunities. We are focused on transforming teaching and learning by creating and scaling digital innovations in three areas: insight, learning, and access.[34]

In March, 2013, inBloom listed 22 partner companies.[35] Most of these were technology companies that hoped to utilize the database for creating personalized online instruction. For example, the inBloom website lists Dell as one of its partners:

> "At Dell we are committed to providing personalized learning solutions to schools, teachers and students around the world. We're happy to be working with inBloom to help move forward this shared vision around innovation through data insight, professional development and creative tools educators need to make personalized learning a reality." Jon Phillips, Global Education Director, Dell Inc.[36]

Another partner, Amazon.com is interested in ensuring the use of its Kindle reader in schools along with providing cloud services:

> "Amazon is excited to work with inBloom to empower teachers with the right tools to manage the digital classroom. With our innovative tools like Whispercast, our vast selection of content, and our cloud solutions from

Amazon Web Services, we hope to drive innovative solutions to improve students' outcomes and lower the costs of education." – Raghu Murthi, VP of Kindle Education & Enterprise.[37]

Capturing the excitement of education technology firms about inBloom at the SXSWedu Conference, Stephanie Simon, reporting for Reuters, declared "Entrepreneurs can't wait" for the newly created national database, which:

already holds files on millions of children identified by name, address and sometimes social security number. Learning disabilities are documented, test scores recorded, attendance noted. In some cases, the database tracks student hobbies, career goals, attitudes toward school – even homework completion.[38]

As noted by the reporter, "federal law allows them (inBloom) to *share files in their portion of the database with private companies selling educational products and services* [author's emphasis]."[39] Besides opening the door for educational entrepreneurs, the new national database generates profits for its creators, the reporter noted, "Amplify Education, a division of Rupert Murdoch's News Corp, built the infrastructure."[40]

Amplify's new 10-inch Android tablet dedicated to classroom use was featured in *The New York Times'* business section. The article captured a network of power and profit between former New York school chancellor Joel Klein and News Corporation's Rupert Murdoch:

On Wednesday at the SXSWedu conference in Austin, Tex., Mr. Klein, the former chancellor of New York City schools and the current chief executive of Amplify, News Corporation's fledgling education division, will take the stage for a surprising announcement. Amplify will not sell just its curriculum on existing tablets, but will also offer the Amplify Tablet, its own 10-inch Android tablet for K–12 schoolchildren.[41]

As Chancellor of the New York school system, Joel Klein originally contracted with the company Wireless Generation, now part of Amplify, to use their data collection and analysis program called "Achievement Reporting and Innovation System (ARIS)." At the time Wireless Generation stated on its website: "Wireless generation . . . builds large-scale data systems that centralize student data and give educators and parents unprecedented visibility into learning."[42] Before being appointed Chancellor of the New York City school system, Joel Klein was a lawyer from ICT conglomerate Bertelsmann. Bertelsmann, which identifies itself as "media worldwide," is composed of six corporate divisions and owns Random House book publishers.[43] Klein lacked the legal requirements to head the New York City schools; New York state law requires substantial education credentials and experience. Consequently, his appointment required a wavier by the New York state commissioner of education.

In 2010, Rupert Murdoch decided to enter the education business by purchasing 90 percent of Wireless Generation for $360 million and hiring Joel Klein to head his new education division. Murdoch, the founder and head of News Corp., expressed his belief in the potential of the education market, "We see a $500 billion sector in the U.S. alone," he said, "that is waiting desperately to be transformed by big breakthroughs that extend the reach of great teaching."[44]

Leaving the chancellorship of the New York Schools to join the for-profit News Corp., Joel Klein highlighted the money to be made investing in educational technology:

> I'll be looking at how to stimulate private investment in what I think are instructional platforms and other technologies I think will change the way K-12 education is delivered. I've got a lot to do before I tell you the details, but that's the basic concept. I think it's going to take substantial private capital to be able to generate the kind of technological advancement I think is absolutely essential.[45]

Announcing Klein's hiring, News Corp. issued a press release: "Mr. Klein will act as a senior advisor to Mr. Murdoch on a wide range of initiatives, including *developing business strategies for the emerging educational marketplace* [author's emphasis]."[46] In the same press release Rupert Murdoch is quoted as saying, "His record [Klein's] of achievement leading one of the country's toughest school systems has given him a unique perspective that will be particularly important as we look into a sector that has long been in need of innovation."[47]

There were complaints about the money Chancellor Klein spent on contracts to for-profit companies. After Klein left New York City, the schools were criticized for its budget problems and an article in *The New York Times* specifically raised concerns about the amount of money paid for Wireless Generation's ARIS. Reporter Sharon Otterman wrote:

> The city comptroller, John C. Liu, announced audits last week of spending on online learning and of the Achievement Reporting and Innovation System, or ARIS, an $80 million school information database that cost more than projected and has been criticized for not living up to its promise of helping schools track student progress effectively.[48]

Wireless Generation proved costly for New York City schools and not very effective. In addition, the school administration was criticized for spending on other tech projects, including $542 million spent on wiring schools and $50 million on contracts for an online course-management system. There were also expenses for hiring Rosetta Stone and Pearson for training and software use. Some schools used Rosetta Stone to teach foreign languages—a substitute for hiring foreign language teachers.[49]

Wireless Generation is also linked to *Education Week* with the Chief Executive Officer of the company, Larry Berger, who retained 10 percent of the ownership after the Rupert purchase, serving on the newspaper's board of trustees. *Education Week* is a major U.S. education newspaper promoting the increasing use of technology in schools through its series "Digital Directions" which is billed as "Tracking news, trends and ideas in educational technology."[50]

As part of Murdoch's Amplify, Wireless Generation offers products and services directly tied to Race to the Top. These include help with instructional improvement using data systems, six computer assessment programs, four curriculum and instruction packages, and five professional services. Among the professional services are four directly related to Race to the Top, namely Data and Instructional Coaching, School Improvement, Common Core Services, Data Use for Professional Development, and Assessment.[51]

Exemplifying how technology companies can make money off Race to the Top, Wireless Generation offers under its Data and Instructional Coaching a service to: "Build teachers' capacity to connect data to everything they do." Besides reflecting an overall belief in data as a key to improving education, the service connects teachers to inBloom through the purchase of hardware or software. A goal is personalizing instruction: "To ensure your teachers know which students to target, the type of instruction needed, and the intensity necessary to increase student achievement."[52] Wireless Generation offers to create in schools a:

> Data Culture: Our coaches are on the ground over an extended period of time leading teams to *connect data, standards, and instruction to student needs* . . . [and a] Data Room: We help school leaders successfully set up and launch a data room, where they conduct regular data meetings that follow an inquiry model of using data to inform decisions [author's emphasis].[53]

The network connections between News Corp., Amplify, Wireless Generation, and *Education Week* were evident in two ads appearing in the March 14, 2013 *Education Week: Technology Count* which listed as a member of its Board of Trustees, "Larry Berger, chief executive officer, Wireless Generation."[54] One ad for Wireless Generation promises that its assessment tool mClass Beacon is "designed to support the increased rigor of the Common Core State Standards."[55] In the same issue, a full page ad for the Amplify tablet states, "you gain a partner focused solely on k-12 education who knows how to integrate the devices into the classroom in meaningful ways."[56]

However, Rupert Murdoch is not the only big player benefiting from the Race to the Top. The other company is Pearson. Similar to Amplify,

Pearson uses student data to individualize instruction with the Knewton adaptive platform. In 2011, Knewton was selected by the World Economic forum as one of 13 pioneers of Information Technology and New Media. Knewton is bringing analytic tools to teachers and students as textbooks become digital and are delivered through e-readers.[57] These analytic tools identify parts of e-textbooks by structure and level of difficulty and connects them to the digital profile of each student. Knewton's website provides this description of its analytic platform:

> How it works
> Knewton is a technology company that uses data to continuously personalize online learning content for individual students. Knewton analyzes data about the performance of each student and similar students on the platform, as well as the relevance of the educational content, in order to serve up the best activity for each student at a particular moment in time.
>
> Continuously adaptive learning
> The platform is continuously *adaptive, meaning it responds in real time to each student's activity on the system and adjusts to provide the most relevant content.* The platform refines its recommendations through network effects that harness the power of all the data collected, for all students, to optimize learning for each individual student [author's emphasis].[58]

Pearson uses the Knewton adaptive learning platform in its product MyLab. On its website, Pearson states:

> The Study Plan or Learning Path in select MyLab titles now features Knewton recommendations. When these recommendations are enabled, Knewton will determine the next best thing for each student to work on as he or she moves through the course.[59]

There are a vast number of other for-profit education companies benefiting from Race to the Top with many of them represented by the lobbying group EIA, which has the mission:

> Conducting advocacy and strategic communications at the Federal, State, and Local levels in support of the role of the private sector in education. This includes ESEA re-authorization, tax incentives for tutoring, regulations/oversight of proprietary schools, and other targeted opportunities that affect the role of the private sector in public education.[60]

EIA clearly states its lobbying goals, EIA "represents the interests of providers when it engages local school officials, States, the US Department of

Education and the Congress. By working together, organizations can amplify their voices with these stakeholder groups so that the special interests of … providers will be better understood."[61]

Making Money in New York

Profit is to be made by selling curricula based on Common Core State Standards. For instance, the New York State Board of Regents in 2013 purchased for $28,335,642 English/Language Arts and mathematics curricula aligned with the Common Core State Standards.[62] The Pre-K2 English/Language curriculum was purchased from the Core Knowledge Foundation, an organization run by E. D. Hirsch, Jr., and, as I will explain in more detail in Chapter 3 on the Republican education agenda, is most often associated with the movement against multiculturalism in the schools.[63] The English/Language curriculum for grades 3–5 was purchased from Expeditionary Learning and for grades 6–8 from Expeditionary Learning under a subcontract with Public Consulting Group. Expeditionary Learning describes itself: "We partner with schools, districts, and charter boards to open new schools and transform existing schools. We provide school leaders and teachers with professional development, curriculum planning resources, and new school structures to boost student engagement, character, and achievement."[64] In 2010, Expeditionary Learning reported working in or running 165 schools in 29 states and Washington, DC.[65]

The Public Consulting Group is an example of a company created primarily to exploit government spending for human services. Besides subcontracting the Expeditionary Learning curriculum, the company also sold to New York the English/Language Arts for grades 9–12.[66] The company describes its services: "Public Consulting Group (PCG) provides industry-leading management consulting and technology to help public sector education, health, human services, and other government clients achieve their performance goals and better serve populations in need."[67] Besides selling restructuring services, the company is benefiting from the Common Core State Standards by selling aligned curriculum packages.

There is money to be made managing charter schools. The National Education Policy Center in its annual report on charter schools for 2010–2011 found that: "The number of states in which for-profit EMOs operated was 33 in 2010–2011. The for-profit education management industry expanded into Alaska and Hawaii this past year for the first time."[68] The report identified the leading for-profit companies operating charter schools and managing public schools:

This year, after the acquisition of KC Distance Learning, K12's total enrollment for its 49 schools (65,396) far exceeds any other EMO. National Heritage Academies' 67 schools come in a far second, with a total enrollment of 42,503. An early leader in the education management industry, Edison Learning, has slipped to fourth in terms of total enrollment, behind Imagine Schools, Inc.[69]

In summary, there is money to be made off Race to the Top.

Race to the Top, Attitudes about Public Schools, and Ideology

In evaluating motives behind Race to the Top it is important to understand the perspective on public schools held by its promoters. By and large, most of the original supporters and implementers of Race to the Top have little public school experience as students, teachers, or administrators. Many attended private schools. Why do the sponsors think Race to the Top will improve the quality of American public schools? Embedded in Race to the Top appears to be a disdain of:

1. traditional public schools (let's have charter schools);
2. locally prepared school curricula (without any research Common Core State Standards are supposed to be an improvement);
3. public school teachers and administrators (value-added testing, again without longitudinal research, is supposed to improve quality of public school teachers and administrators);
4. college teacher education programs (considered intellectual slumming).

All of the original promoters of Race to the Top attended Ivy League colleges, mostly Harvard. Many are associated with investment banking. In other words, when examining the educational backgrounds of the advocates of Race to the Top it is easy to conclude that they have an elite perspective on public schools.

Consider the educational background of the main spokesperson for Race to the Top, U.S. Secretary of Education Arne Duncan. He is private school educated, a graduate of Harvard, and a professional basketball player.[70] Born November 6, 1964, he attended and graduated from the private University of Chicago Laboratory Schools and then went to Harvard majoring in sociology. At Harvard, Duncan co-captained the varsity basketball team and from 1987 to 1991 played professional basketball in Australia. In 1992, childhood friend and investment banker John W. Rogers, Jr. appointed Duncan director of the Ariel Education Initiative, a mentoring program for inner-city children. After the school closed in 1996, Duncan and Rogers were instrumental in re-opening it as the Ariel Community Academy, a charter school. In 1999, Duncan was appointed Deputy Chief of Staff for Chicago Public Schools and in 2001 became Chief Executive Officer of the Chicago Public Schools. He held this position until being appointed Secretary of Education in 2008.[71]

It's hard to explain Duncan's rapid rise from professional basketball player to head of the Chicago school system after only eight years running a mentoring program and working in a charter school. One possible explanation could be the support of investment banker John W. Rogers, Jr., who possibly shared the same ideological views as the investment bankers that formed the Democrats for Education Reform. It's important to note that Duncan did not have any education or experience to even qualify as a school principal let alone Chief Executive Officer of the entire Chicago public school system.

Certainly, the goals of the Ariel Community Academy seem to reflect the perspective of investment bankers about what children from low-income families need. "We want to make the stock market a topic of dinner table conversation," proclaimed a headline splashed across the page of a brochure for the Ariel Community Academy serving students from low-income Chicago families. The school continued to be supported by Duncan when he became Chief Executive Officer of the Chicago Public Schools and he continued to serve on the school's Board of Directors.[72]

Ironically, at the time of the 2008 collapse of several U.S. investment institutions, including Lehman Brothers whose personnel spent time at the Academy working as part of the Saturday Morning Teacher Corps, the Ariel Community Academy used an investment curriculum in which "students study commerce, trade and the growth of business around the world." First graders were given $20,000 to invest in a class stock portfolio.[73] Each graduating class was to return the original $20,000 investment to the entering first grade and donate half the profits to the school with the rest distributed among the graduating students.[74]

Embedded in the philosophy of Ariel Community Academy was the argument used by investment firms discussed in the previous section, namely that education can end poverty. In addition, the very actions of the school seemed to indicate that if children from low-income families learned to invest they would be able to escape poverty. On the website for Ariel Investments, their charter school is described as "unique corporate-family-school partnership ... where financial literacy is not just taught but practiced."[75] If anything, the financial collapse of 2008 may have taught these low-income students to not trust investment bankers or the stock market.

Similar to Arne Duncan and the Ariel Community Academy, Duncan's supporters in the Democrats for Education Reform were all tied to investment banking. One of the three founding members, John Petry, graduated from the prestigious University of Pennsylvania's Wharton School of Finance and in 2005, when the Democrats for Education Reform was founded, he was a partner at Gotham Capital where he remained until 2010.[76] The United Federation of Teachers, New York City's teachers' union and critic of the

Race to the Top agenda, provided this description of Petry as a board member of Democrats for Education Reform:

> John Petry, a partner at Gotham Capital Management, chairs the board of Education Reform Now. Petry's Gotham Capital LLC, founded in 1985 with $7 million from junk-bond king Michael Milken, is a privately owned hedge fund that manages investments for wealthy clients, investing in equities as well as spin-offs, restructuring and takeovers.[77]

Whitney Tilson, another founder of Democrats for Education Reform, attended Stanford's Bing Nursery School and the private Northfield Mt. Hermon School in Mount Hermon, Massachusetts. He graduated from Harvard College in 1989 and the Harvard Business School in 1994. He co-founded the Value Investment Congress described as: "The Value Investing Congress is the place for value investors from around the world to network with other serious, sophisticated value investors and benefit from the sharing of investment wisdom."[78] As founder and member of the Board of Directors of Democrats for Education Reform, their website describes him as:

> Whitney Tilson – Managing Partner, T2 Partners LLC and Tilson Mutual Funds; Board member of KIPP-NYC, National Alliance for Public Charter Schools and Council of Urban Professionals; Co-Founder of the Initiative for a Competitive Inner City and Rewarding Achievement (REACH).[79]

The third co-founder of Democrats for Education Reform is described on their website: "Boykin Curry – Eagle Capital; Co-Founder of Public Prep."[80] It was at Curry's apartment that the Democrats for Education Reform met with Senator Barack Obama in 2005 to discuss education policy.[81] Brill describes Curry, his full name is Ravenal Boykin Curry, as a "typical preppie socialite" who "went to Yale and Harvard Business School ... [and] the regular memos on the economy that he sends his investors, [shows] Curry's interest in education reform was serious and sophisticated."[82]

Even President Barack Obama has little experience with public schools. He attended a private elite school and Ivy League colleges. Except for a brief period attending a public school in Honolulu before moving to Indonesia at the age of six, President Obama never attended a public school or taught in one. After returning from Indonesia in 1971, he entered fifth grade at the exclusive Hawaiian private school Punahou graduating in 1979. He then attended Occidental and Columbia University before going on to Harvard Law School where he graduated magna cum laude in 1991.[83] There is little, if nothing, in his educational background to help him understand the inner workings of public schools.

Limited school experience seems to be a characteristic of those in the for-profit education industry. For instance, in previous discussions it was noted that Klein was a lawyer before being appointed Chancellor of the New York City school system. Unlike those discussed so far in this section, Klein actually attended public schools, graduating from William Cullen Bryant High School in Queens, New York in 1963, and then attended Columbia University and Harvard Law School, where he earned his law degree in 1971. He clerked in federal courts and worked in the White House Counsel's under President Clinton. He then became Counsel to Bertelsmann before being appointed by Mayor Michael Bloomberg to be Chancellor of the New York City schools.[84]

Technically, Klein, along with his future replacement, Hearst Corporation executive Cathleen Black appointed Chancellor in 2010, had no professional educational background and lacked the legal requirements to head the New York City schools. Mayor Michael Bloomberg explained why he would be a good choice despite Klein's limited school experience:

> He has the leadership skills. He has the intergovernmental skills. He has the feeling and compassion for people. He is incorruptible. He is a visionary. And I believe that he will deliver to this city what we promised, a quality education for all of our children.[85]

The New York Times reported:

> Because Mr. Klein has no experience in school administration, a waiver will be required from the Department of Education in Albany. But Mr. Bloomberg said he was confident that the waiver would be granted. "If the scholarship and background requirements that Joel Klein has doesn't pass," the mayor said, "nobody would pass".[86]

Probably nothing better expresses elitist views about schools then Mayor Bloomberg's appointment of Cathleen Black as Chancellor. Her major accomplishment was pioneering the publication of *USA Today* for the Hearst Corporation. Reporter Jeremy Peters noted that, "Schools Chief Has Much in Common With Boss," because of her background as the head of Hearst Corporation's magazine division since 1979.[87] It was reported that she "moved in the same Upper East Side [New York City] circles as the billionaire mayor" and, it could be assumed, the founders of Democrats for Education Reform.[88] She admitted that she wasn't qualified for the position:

> A day after her surprise ouster as New York City's top education official, Cathleen P. Black acknowledged that she was ill-prepared for the demands and visibility of running the nation's largest public school system. "It was like having to learn Russian in a weekend," Ms. Black said, "and then give

speeches in Russian and speak Russian in budget committee and City Council meetings".[89]

She lasted only three months and gained some fame for responding to parents' concerns about crowded schools with the quip, "Could we just have some birth control for a while?"[90]

Michelle Rhee is another person widely hailed in the reform movement who rapidly rose to a position of education power. Rhee did attend public schools until the sixth grade and then, after a year in South Korea, her parents enrolled her in the private Maumee Valley Country Day School from which she graduated in 1988. She then received a B.A in government from Cornell University and master's degree in public policy from Harvard University's John F. Kennedy School of Government. After a five-week training course with Teach For America, she taught for three years in the Baltimore public school system. In 1997, after graduating from Harvard, the founder of Teach For America, Wendy Koop, asked her to run a nonprofit corporation, The New Teacher Project. In 2007, she was appointed Chancellor of the Washington, DC school system without any experience or education as a school administrator.

Oddly, most of the people described in this section have only limited or no experience attending or teaching in public schools. None in this group ever enrolled in a teacher education program or a graduate program in school administration even though some served as superintendents or chancellors of major school systems and one became U.S. Secretary of Education. They all graduated from elite private universities. Given their elite educational backgrounds and lack of public school experience, one can wonder why they think they have the best ideas on how to change public schools. The more cynical might say that their elitist backgrounds might result in them being biased against teacher education programs, public school teachers' status, public school administrators, public school curricula, and teachers' unions. A more positive statement might be that they are do-gooders using hard evidence to improve public schooling. However, this positive statement must be qualified by the lack of longitudinal research supporting Common Core State Standards and the rather weak findings on teacher education programs and evaluation procedures.

In summary, the ideological perspectives of investment firms, for-profit education industries, and those described in this section include:

1. a belief that traditional public schools are failures;
2. a belief that the traditional education bureaucracy is an impediment to meaningful change as compared to the work of for-profit education companies;
3. a belief that unions, particularly teachers' unions, are hurting education and the economy;

4.   a belief that the growing inequality of income is a result of a poor public school system and that education "reform" is the answer to American economic problems;
5.   a belief that charter schools, and not traditional public schools, will better serve children from low-income families;
6.   a rejection of racial and economic integration of schools as an important means of reducing inequality of educational opportunity.

Economists Take Charge: Alternative Teacher Certification and Evaluation

Research questioning the value of teacher education programs and public school evaluations systems primarily comes from economists, particularly Harvard Professor Thomas Kane and Stanford University, Hoover Institute's Eric Hanushek. As I discussed in Chapter 1, human capital economists are behind most of the rhetoric that changing public schools will improve the U.S. economy and make the U.S. more competitive against other global economies. I asserted in Chapter 1 that despite claims of human capital economists, there is no longitudinal research that convincingly shows changing schools will improve America's ability to compete in world markets or reduce inequality of incomes.

An example of these kinds of economic assertions can be found in a report crucial to the Race to the Top's agenda for value-added teaching and alternatives to traditional teacher certification. This report and its recommendations were discussed in Chapter 1: *Identifying Effective Teachers Using Performance on the Job.*[91] Similar to our previous discussion of investor reports, the Hamilton Project claims that "education has become a constraint on future productivity growth and a root cause of income inequality."[92] There is no footnote or other citation provided for this assertion!

The report's authors, Robert Gordon, Thomas J. Kane, and Douglas Staiger, are all economists who are part of a network linked to the Democrats for Education Reform. At the time of the report's publication, Robert Gordon was Senior Vice President for Economic Policy, Center for American Progress and Associate Director for Education, Income Maintenance, and Labor in the Office of Budget and Management.[93] Douglas Staiger was an economist at Dartmouth College.[94] And most importantly, the third author and pioneer in the work of value-added evaluations of teachers, Thomas J. Kane, is Professor of Education and Economics at the Harvard Graduate School of Education and was from 1991 through 2000 a faculty member at the Kennedy School of Government.[95]

Their assertion that education is the root cause of income inequality and claims that higher levels of credentialing are required by the labor market is not supported by employment projections by the U.S. Bureau of Labor Statistics. In fact, increasing educational levels of the population might result in educational inflation or brain waste, such as college graduates being unemployed or working as waiters and cooks. The U.S. Bureau of Labor Statistics' Occupational Outlook Handbook states for the period 2010–2020 that:

> Total employment is expected to increase by 20.5 million jobs from 2010 to 2020, with 88 percent of detailed occupations projected to experience employment growth. Industries and occupations related to *health care, personal care and social assistance, and construction* are projected to have the fastest job growth between 2010 and 2020 [author's emphasis].[96]

According to their projections, the top two fastest growing occupations, personal care aides and home health aides, require: "Entry-level Education: Less than high school."[97] The next fastest growing job sector, medical secretaries, requires a high school diploma or equivalent. In 2013, the National Association of Home Builders announced:

> March 21, 2013 – Growing labor shortages in all facets of the residential construction sector are impeding the housing and economic recovery, according to a new survey conducted by the National Association of Home Builders (NAHB). The survey of our members shows that since June of 2012, residential construction firms are reporting an increasing number of shortages in all aspects of the industry – from carpenters, excavators, framers, roofers and plumbers, to bricklayers, HVAC, building maintenance managers and weatherization workers.[98]

According to the Bureau of Labor Statistics, these jobs require less than a high school diploma or a high school diploma or its equivalent.[99]

The authors' assertion, without any supporting reference, that education is the solution to income inequality is similar to that of previously discussed investment reports. It seems like more of a hope than based on any realities of the job market. A similar issue arises when they report on the differences between teachers with and without teaching credentials. This is a key argument in the criticism of teacher training programs and the push for alternative forms of certification.

The three economists assert: "Controlling for baseline characteristics of students and comparing classrooms within schools, there is no statistically significant difference in achievement for students assigned to certified and uncertified teachers."[100] Based on this assertion, they argue, "that there is no reason to limit initial entrance into teaching to those who have completed traditional certification programs or are willing to take such courses in their first years on the job."[101]

The citation for the claim of no statistical difference between certified and noncertified teachers is an unpublished paper.[102] This unpublished paper is limited to two cohorts of elementary school teachers hired by the Los Angeles school district in the 1995–1996 and 1996–1997 school year when many uncertified teachers were being hired because of a teacher shortage. The authors' conclusion uses the word "suggesting" and not "proof" in comparing teacher effectiveness: "The absence of any impact on student achievement is consistent with our cross-sectional results, *suggesting* certified teachers were no more effective than the uncertified [author's emphasis]."[103] Student test scores were used to evaluate teacher effectiveness. However, they eliminated from the study students who switched teachers during the course of a year, students with disabilities, and students in "classrooms with extraordinarily large (more than 36) or extraordinarily small (less than 10)."[104]

Besides cherry-picking the students, a closer look at their results suggests that credentialed teachers performed better than noncredentialed teachers. For example, they found: "Within a given school, grade, calendar track and academic year, the students assigned to less experienced and uncertified teachers appear to perform poorly relative to those assigned to traditionally certified teachers."[105]

Not to belabor the point, it does seem odd that an unpublished research study based on two school years in one city would result in a conclusion that being a credentialed teacher made no difference in student learning and resulted in a policy recommendation to "Reduce the barriers to entry into teaching for those without traditional teacher certification."[106]

The 2006 Hamilton Project continues to be cited to justify value-added and alternative forms of certification. For instance, Michelle Rhee's The New Teacher Project, formed in 1997 with Teach For America, continues to cite the 2006 study. Their 2010 report "Teacher Evaluation 2.0" has on its opening page a quote from the Hamilton Project's study: "Having a top-quartile teacher rather than a bottom-quartile teacher four years in a row could be enough to close the black-white test score gap. Gordon, Kane and Staiger, 2006."[107] Among several evaluation methods, the report proposes: "Whenever possible, these should include objective measures of student academic growth, such as value-added models that connect students' progress on standardized assessments to individual teachers while controlling for important factors such as students' academic history."[108]

The claim that teacher evaluation is one key to reducing the disparity in "black-white" test scores and inequalities of income, matches the concerns found in the previously discussed investment reports. Again it shifts the burden of economic problems, inequalities of income and economic growth, to the public schools. By presenting this argument it counters the possibility of changing the tax system or other government policies to reduce income disparities. It also protects wealthier public school districts from plans for economic integration of poor and wealthy school districts by claiming schools serving low-income students will improve through changes in teacher credentialing and evaluation. In other words, a result of the economic arguments regarding teachers presented in this section is to protect the rich.

No Child Left Behind, Race to the Top and Economic Segregation

There is strong evidence that No Child Left Behind and Race to the Top protect school districts and schools serving upper-income students rather than schools serving students from low-income families. Writing in *The New York Times* on May 19, 2012, David Kirp, Professor of Public Policy at the University of California, Berkley, argued:

> The failure of the No Child Left Behind regimen to narrow the achievement gap offers the sobering lesson that closing underperforming public schools, setting high expectations for students, getting tough with teachers and opening a raft of charter schools isn't the answer. If we're serious about improving educational opportunities, we need to revisit the abandoned policy of school integration.[109]

Economic and racial segregation have increased, as reported in 2012 by the UCLA Civil Rights Project.[110] With the descriptive title "E Pluribus ... Deepening Double Segregation for More Students," the report concludes:

> Segregation has increased dramatically across the country for Latino students, who are attending more intensely segregated and impoverished schools than they have for generations ... In spite of declining residential segregation for black families and large-scale movement to the suburbs in most parts of the country, school segregation remains very high for black students. It is also double segregation by both race and poverty.[111]

Racial and economic segregation for Latino students has increased since the 2001 No Child Left Behind legislation:

> In the early 2000s, the average Latino and black student attended a school where a *little over half of the students* were low income (as measured by free and reduced price lunch eligibility), but now attend schools where low income students account for *nearly two-thirds of their classmates* [author's emphasis].[112]

The report asserts that segregation is a major cause of school failure:

> The consensus of nearly sixty years of social science research on the harms of school segregation is clear: separate remains extremely unequal. Schools of concentrated poverty and segregated minority schools are strongly related to an array of factors that limit educational opportunities and outcomes.[113]

From the standpoint of the UCLA Civil Rights Project, Race to the Top has passively allowed increased segregation resulting in "severely limit[ing] educational opportunities for African American and Latino students, as well as the opportunity for all students to learn to live and work effectively in a multiracial society."[114]

The UCLA Civil Rights Project lends support to the argument that an implicit reason for supporting for No Child Left Behind and Race to the Top is to protect the educational privileges of public schools and school districts serving upper-income families. This might be considered an unwarranted suggestion since so much of the rhetoric surrounding these two pieces of legislation claims they will enhance educational opportunities for children from low-income families. The report states: "More recently ... the Bush and Obama Administrations have vigorously fostered policies that reflected their passive attitude toward resegregation issues."[115]

Teach For America, The New Teacher Project, and Teacher Training and Evaluation

The justification and networks created by Wendy Kopp's Teach For America supported policies related to alternative forms of certification, anti-teacher unionism, and new forms of teacher evaluation. The networks created by Teach For America include the Democrats for Education Reform, Joel Klein (former New York Chancellor and now head of Murdoch's Amplify), charter schools, investment firms, foundations, and The New Teacher Project.

Conceived in 1989 in Wendy Kopp's senior thesis at Princeton University, Teach For America planned to send the "best" college graduates to schools serving low-income students to work for two years. The hope was that these volunteers would improve the education of low-income students and after leaving the program would continue to work to improve public schools. Three of the graduates of the program, Michelle Rhee, Dave Levin, and Whitney Tilson, did have a profound effect on the school reform movement with Rhee becoming the controversial school chancellor of Washington, DC, Levin founding the national network of KIPP (Knowledge is Power) charter schools, and Tilson helping to found the Democrats for Education Reform.

Inherent in Kopp's thesis and Teach For America was a criticism of public school teachers, public schools, and teacher training institutions. It was assumed that the so-called "best" college graduates from the "best" schools could be trained in one summer session to teach low-income students. In other words, potential teachers did not need a certificate from a teacher training institution to work in some of the most difficult schools in the U.S. Kopp wrote, "If top recent college graduates devoted two years to teaching in public schools, they could have a real impact on the lives of disadvantaged kids."[116] After two years of teaching experience, she asserted:

> They would become business leaders and newspaper editors, U.S. senators and Supreme Court justices, community leaders and school board members. And, because of their experience teaching in public schools, they would make decisions that would change them for the better.[117]

After graduating, Kopp describes how her Princeton credentials opened doors and gained her financial support for organizing Teach For America. Not surprisingly, those believing teachers needed extensive training were, in her words, "reluctant to invest in Teach For America, whose recruits would go through only a short pre-service training program before entering the classroom."[118] These critics wanted, she wrote, to focus on improving teacher training programs. She dismissed this concern with the argument that these "best" recent college graduates "would be caring people who would go above and beyond to meet their students' needs and who would be driven to learn from their students, their students' families, and their colleagues."[119]

So the "best" students from the "best" colleges were going to improve and maybe save public school children from low-income families. Embodied in this idea were negative attitudes about public school teachers and traditional schools. This negative attitude was best expressed in a speech by Ray Owens, a corps member, given at the 1990 closing ceremony for the first summer training session. Kopp wrote, "What he said moved me greatly," and she proudly put the speech in her book.[120] Referring to public schools and children from low-income families, Owens said, "The monsters of educational failure have locked them into the dismal dens of ignorance and despair. They have internalized the low level of expectation and inferiority that many of this nation's school systems have designed and perpetuated for them."[121]

One could label his remarks elitist based on the statement that followed the above quote. When I read the statement below, I wondered how many students in 1990 attended schools that offered courses in literary analysis and calculus—my middle class high school didn't offer these courses.

> The nation that promises "liberty and justice for all" has failed these children by sending them to schools that don't offer courses in calculus and literary analysis, courses that they will need in order to prepare for the demanding coursework of our institutions of higher learning.[122]

The content of the first training program was patched together just a few months before it began. How well did Teach For America prepare its teachers to help students who might have social and psychological problems, and might need special help such as English language learners? An example of how good the preparation was can be found in the autobiography of one of its more famous alumnus Michelle Rhee.

Rhee entered Teach For America after graduating from Cornell and, as described earlier, before entering Harvard. In 1992, she received training during the summer at California State University at Northridge before being sent to Baltimore to teach second grade in an area she described as a "very downtrodden, dangerous neighborhood."[123] Of course, the short training period, in fact, did not provide adequate preparation for teaching. "My class," she wrote, "was infamous at a school that had experienced its share of violence and misbehavior ... 'That's Rhee's class,' the other teachers would say, with palpable distaste."[124] After returning the first year from a Christmas visit with her parents, she admitted her lack of training and wrote about the period:

> My new strategy was to throw spaghetti against the wall, hoping some-thing would stick. I tried everything ... If one system didn't work, I'd introduce another a few days later. The constant changes weren't good for the kids, but I was a woman possessed. I was bent on figuring out a way to be successful.[125]

She saw another teacher's room as "a model of organization and preparation."[126] Her recounting of the first year teaching is not an endorsement for Wendy Kopp's belief that low-income students could be saved by, after a short training period, putting in the best college students from the best schools.

Rhee taught for three years before leaving and heading for Harvard. By the end of the third year, she felt she had become a competent teacher as opposed to the first year when "the savviest parents took their kids of out of my classroom. They knew my classroom was out of control."[127]

In 1997, when Wendy Kopp asked her to organize The New Teacher Project, Rhee had only three years of teaching experience. Funded by the Gap Inc., Rhee was given a desk at the Wall Street headquarters of Teach For America. Rhee's idea was for school districts to sign contracts for The New Teacher Project to supply teachers. It was during a time of a major teacher shortage and school dis-tricts were begging for teachers. Different from Teach For America, Rhee's program targeted people who wanted to change careers and enter teaching. Her first two contracts were with the Philadelphia and Austin schools. In New York City, she started a Teaching Fellows program. Eventually, her contracts with school districts extended across the country.[128]

Her anti-teachers' union attitudes developed over frustrations in placing teachers in schools. Rhee wrote critically about union rules that protected teachers from dismissals and seniority rules. Her criticism of teachers' unions got the attention of the new Chancellor of the New York City school system, Joel Klein. At the time, The New Teacher Project was the largest supplier of new teachers to the New York City schools. Rhee wrote, "I loved Joel Klein from the moment I first spoke with him."[129] In the acknowledgement to her 2013 book, she wrote, "And finally, I owe a debt to my mentors: Joel Klein, thank you for having more confidence in me than I do myself at times."[130] Of particular interest is a stated debt to David Coleman, the architect of the Common Core State Standards.[131]

Similar to Arne Duncan's meteoric rise to the U.S. Department of Education, Rhee, with three years of teaching experience, ten years directing The New Teacher Project, and no experience in school administration, was appointed Chancellor of the Washington, DC schools. She lasted less than three years and left under considerable controversy to form StudentsFirst: A Movement to Transform Public Education with the endorsement of Joel Klein:

> Michelle Rhee will bring demonstrated excellence backed by enormous energy and commitment to the national discussion on school reform. What she did in Washington, D.C. was game changing, which is precisely what the country needs—bold leadership that is unafraid to put students first, regardless how controversial that may prove to be to those who continue to protect a status quo that fails children.—*Joel I. Klein, outgoing New York City Schools Chancellor*[132]

Klein continues to serve on the Board of Directors of StudentsFirst.[133]

StudentsFirst advocates the same teacher policies as Democrats for Education Reform and other groups described in this chapter, and the policies in Race to the Top. The organization is campaigning to "Evaluate teachers based on evidence of student results [value-added]" and "Pay teachers based on their impact on student results."[134] It also calls for alternative paths for teacher certification and maximizing parents' choice of schools, particularly charter schools.

Two other graduates of Teach For America, Dave Levin and Mike Feinberg, ushered in the era of charter schools as part of a War on Poverty. They founded the KIPP (Knowledge is Power) network of charter schools with initial funding from Gap Inc. Reflecting the philosophy embedded in Teach For America that traditional public schools failed to help children from low-income families, KIPP academies use a combination of character training, academic study, and long hours. By 2013, the KIPP network served more than 41,000 students in 125 schools in 20 states (plus Washington, DC) across the country.[135] According to the National Policy Center report, KIPP is the largest of the nonprofit education management companies and that in 2010–2011 it "experienced the largest net increase in schools during the past school year, from 82 to 102 schools."[136] Between 2011 and 2013, the number of KIPP schools increased from 102 to 125 and is still growing. Certainly, Race to the Top by promoting charter schools has added to the growth of this attempt to solve the problem of educating students from low-income homes.

In summary, Teach For America spawned a set of ideas that rejected traditional teacher training, launched attacks on teachers' unions, promoted value-added evaluation of teachers, supported the idea that education can solve the problem of poverty, and rejected traditional public schools as inadequate for low-income students. Graduates of Teach For America can be found in policy groups, foundations, and for-profit education companies associated with Race to the Top policies.

Conclusion

A summary and interrelationships of people, venture philanthropies, think tanks, for-profit companies, and investment bankers associated with Race to the Top can be found in Figure 2.1 and Table 2.1. Figure 2.1 shows the linkages between the Democrats for Education Reform, President Barack Obama, U.S. Secretary of Education Arne Duncan, and Race to the Top. In addition, Figure 2.1 contains tables showing the basic policies of Democrats for Education Reform, the groups supporting and benefitting from Race to the Top and their general attitudes and motivations. Table 2.1 lists the major players in promoting Race to the Top policies, including investment bankers, major for-profit companies, venture philanthropy and think tanks, mergers and acquisitions in the for-profit education industry, and major human capital economists.

Notes

1 David Sirota, "Stop Pretending Wealthy CEOs Pushing For Charter Schools Are Altruistic 'Reformers'. They're Raking in Billions," Salon.com. Retrieved from http://www.salon.com/2013/03/11/getting_rich_off_of_schoolchildren/on March 12, 2013.
2 Stephanie Simon, "K-12 Student Database Jazzes Tech Startups, Spooks Parents," Reuters (March 3, 2013). Retrieved from http://www.reuters.com/assets/print?aid=USBRE92204W20130303 on March 5, 2013.
3 Tom Vander Ark, "Private Capital and Public Education: Toward Quality At Scale," AEI Future of American Education Project Working Paper 2009-02, American Enterprise Institute (Washington, DC: American Enterprise Institute, 2009).
4 Learn Capital, "Team." Retrieved from http://www.learncapital.com/team/on March 15, 2013.
5 Learn Capital, "Portfolio." Retrieved from http://www.learncapital.com/portfolio/ on March 21, 2013.
6 Fredrick M. Hess, "Foreword" to Tom Vander Ark, "Private Capital and Public Education: Toward Quality At Scale," AEI Future of American Education Project Working Paper 2009-02, American Enterprise Institute (Washington, DC: American Enterprise Institute, 2009).
7 Ark, "Private Capital and Public Education," p. 1.
8 Ibid.
9 Michael T. Moe, Matthew P. Hanson, Li Jang, and Luben Pampoulov, *American Revolution 2.0: How Education Innovation is Going to Revitalize America and Transform the U.S. Economy* (Woodside, CA: GSV Asset Management, July 4, 2012).

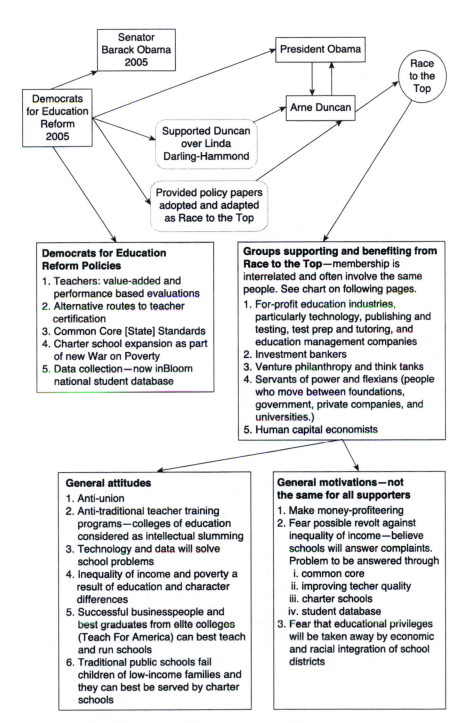

FIGURE 2.1   The Political Coup Known as Race to the Top.

TABLE 2.1 Roadmap to Power in School Reform Movement

Servants of Power and Flexians[1] (Many with little or no public school experience before reaching leadership role in education)	Investment Bankers	Major for-profit Companies (too many companies to list all)	Venture Philanthropy and Think Tanks	Major Mergers and Acquisitions (too many to list all)	Key Human Capital Economists
Barack Obama Arne Duncan Joel Klein Michelle Rhee Wendy Kopp Founders of Democrats for Education Reform 1. Boykin Curry 2. Whitney Tilson 3. John Petry John Schnur Thomas Kane edTPA 1. Linda Darling-Hammond (Stanford)	Democrats for Education Reform 1. Boykin Curry—Eagle Capital 2. Whitney Tilson—Managing Partner, T2 Partners LLC and Tilson Mutual Funds 3. John Petry—Gotham Capital Learn Capital lists 28 for-profit education companies	Education Industry Association (lobbying group for for-profit education companies) Amplify: News Corp.—Rupert Murdoch and Joel Klein 1. inBloom national public school data system 2. Amplify tablet 3. Wireless Generation (Data analytics) Pearson: the leading pre K-12 curriculum, testing, and software company in the U.S. 1. Pearson School Systems: 50% of U.S. schools use at least one of our student curriculum, instructional management and financial software packages. 2. My Lab-Knewton Adaptive Learning Platform 3. edTPA 4. Pearson Early Learning 5. Pearson Digital Learning	Bill and Melinda Gates Foundation Broad Foundation Walton Family Foundation Pearson 1. Pearson Foundation Fordham American Enterprise Institute Manhattan Institute for Policy Research National Council on Teacher Quality StudentsFirst (Michelle Rhee) Teach For America	Pearson 1. eCollege.com ($504 million) 2. Connections Academy ($400 million) 3. Schoolnet ($230 million) New Corp. (Murdoch)—Wireless Generation ($430 million) Advent, Bain Berkshire Partners, Stockbridge—Skillsoft ($1.1 billion)	Value-Added Teacher Evaluations 1. Thomas Kane (Harvard) 2. Robert Gordon (University of California—San Diego) 3. Douglas Staiger (Dartmouth College) Teacher Value Studies—Eric Hanushek—Hoover Institution, Stanford Preschool traits for economic success—James

| 2. Sharon Robinson (AACTE) 3. Raymond Pecheone (Stanford) | GSV Capital - *American Revolution 2.0: How Education Innovation is Going to Revitalize America and Transform the U.S. Economy.* | 6. Family Education Network. 7. Elementary—Pearson Scott Foresman 8. Secondary—Pearson Prentice Hall Test Prep and Tutoring 1. Sylvan 2. Kumon 3. Kaplan 4. Princeton Review Apple iPad, Apps, iTunes U Microsoft-software, education technologies, Surface tablet Dell-data management, instructional technology MacMillan New Ventures Cengage Desire2Learn Houghton Mifflin Harcourt HMH Fuse Scholastic KidZui For-profit charter school companies (too many to name) Blackboard: Moddlerooms and NetSpot | The New Teacher Project Student Achievement Project Foundation for Excellence in Education (Jeb Bush) Core Knowledge Foundation | Promethean-Raycliff Capital, Vantage Partners-SynapticMash ($13 million) | Heckman University of Chicago—Noble Prize 2000 Claims education will improve the economy and reduce inequality of incomes (James Heckman (University of Chicago Noble prize), Alan Krueger (Princeton) and other human capital economists) |

Attitudes	Attitudes	Attitudes
1. School reform will reduce inequality of income and poverty	1. Profitmaking from private companies selling to public schools	1. Believe technology and data will improve schooling 2. Profitmaking

(*Continued*)

TABLE 2.1 (Continued)

Servants of Power and Flexians[1] (Many with little or no public school experience before reaching leadership role in education)	Investment Bankers	Major for-profit Companies (too many to list all)	Venture Philanthropy and Think Tanks	Major Mergers and Acquisitions (too many to list all)	Key Human Capital Economists
2. Do not advocate economic or racial integration of schools 3. Better teachers and charter schools will reduce poverty and income inequalities 4. Negative attitudes about traditional teacher education programs 5. Anti–union	2. School reform will reduce inequality of income and poverty 3. Do not advocate economic or racial integration of schools 4. Better teachers and charter schools will reduce poverty and income inequalities 5. Negative attitudes about traditional teacher education programs 6. Anti–union				

1 Flexian: A person who moves between positions in government, foundations, and private companies

10 GSV Capital, "Management Team." Retrieved from http://gsvcap.com/management/ on March 16, 2013.

11 Moe, et al., *American Revolution 2.0*, pp. 19, 25.

12 Ibid., p. 24.

13 Ibid., p. 25.

14 Ibid., p. 25.

15 Ibid., p. 25.

16 Ibid., p. 25.

17 Ibid., p. 47.

18 Ibid., p. 48.

19 Ibid., p. 48.

20 Ibid., p. 48.

21 Ibid., pp. 48–49.

22 Gary Miron, Jessica L. Urschel, Mayra A. Yat Aguilar, and Breanna Dailey, *Profiles of For-Profit and Nonprofit Education Management Organizations: Thirteenth Annual Report – 2010–2011* (Boulder, CO: School of Education, University of Colorado Boulder, National Education Policy Center, January 2012).

23 U.S. Department of Education, "Race to the Top Program: Executive Summary," p. 2.

24 Council of Chief State School Officers, "Shared Learning Collaborative Background." Retrieved from http://www.ccsso.org/Resources/Programs/Shared_Learning_Collaborative_(SLC).html on March 12, 2013.

25 Ibid.

26 See Anthony G. Picciano and Joel Spring, *The Great American Education-Industrial Complex: Ideology, Technology, and Profit* (New York: Routledge, 2013), pp. 119–143.

27 Council of Chief State School Officers, "Supporting Organizations and Partners." Retrieved from http://www.ccsso.org/Resources/Programs/Shared_Learning_Collaborative_(SLC).html on March 12, 2013.

28 inBloom, "About." Retrieved from https://www.inbloom.org/about-inbloom on March 12, 2013.

29 inBloom, "Our Vision." Retrieved from https://www.inbloom.org/our-vision on March 12, 2013.

30 Ibid.

31 Ibid.

32 Ibid.

33 SXSWedu Conference and Festival, March 4–7, 2013, Austin, Texas. Retrieved from http://sxswedu.com/ on March 11, 2013.

34 "Sponsors, SXSWedu Conference and Festival, March 4–7, 2013, Austin, Texas, "Sponsors." Retrieved from http://sxswedu.com/sxswedu-2013-sponsors on March 11, 2013.

35 Ibid.

36 inBloom, "Providers." Retrieved from https://www.inbloom.org/providers on March 12, 2013.

37 Ibid.

38 Stephanie Simon, "K-12 Student Database Jazzes Tech Startups, Spooks Parents."

39 Ibid.

40 Ibid.

41 Amy Chozick, "News Corp. Has a Tablet for Schools" *The New York Times* (March 6, 2013). Retrieved from http://www.nytimes.com/2013/03/06/business/media/news-corp-has-a-tablet-for-schools.html?ref=todayspaper&_r=0&pagewanted=print on March 6, 2013.

42 Wireless Generation, "About Wireless Generation." Retrieved from http://www.wgen.net/about-us/about.html on December 15, 2010.

43 Bertelsmann: Media Worldwide, "A Company and its Divisions." Retrieved from http://www.bertelsmann.com/bertelsnann_corp/wms41/brn/index.php?ci=99& language=2 on January 6, 2008.

44 Ian Quillen, "Rupert Murdoch Moves Into k-12 Tech. Market," *Education Week* (December 8, 2010), p. 16.

45 Katie Ash, "Klein Touts Tech as He Leaves NYC Schools," *Education Week* (November 12, 2010). Retrieved from http://blogs.edweek.org/edweek/DigitalEducation/2010/11/securing_private_capital_for_n.html on July 8, 2013.

46 Press Release, "News Corporation Appoints Former New York City Department of Education Chancellor Joel Klein as Executive Vice President, Office of the Chairman, News Corporation (November 9, 2010)." Retrieved from http://www.newscorp.com/news/news_462.html on March 22, 2011.

47 See News Corporation's "2010 Annual Report" for a listing of companies. Retrieved from http://newscorp.com/report2010/ar2010.pdf on July 8, 2013.

48 Sharon Otterman, "Amid Layoffs, City to Spend More on School Technology," *The New York Times* (March 29, 2011). Retrieved from http://www.nytimes.com/2011/03/30/nyregion/30schools.html?_r=1&ref=todayspaper&pagewanted=print on March 29, 2011.

49 Ibid.

50 Sarah Sparks, "When Joel Klein resigned as Chancellor in 2010 he accepted a position as Executive Vice President at Wireless Generation."

51 Wireless Generation, Part of Amplify. Retrieved from http://www.wirelessgeneration.com/ on March 15, 2013.

52 Wireless Generation, "Data and Instructional Coaching." Retrieved from http://www.wirelessgeneration.com/services/coaching on March 15, 2013.

53 Ibid.

54 "Board of Trustees, Editorial Projects in Education," *Education Week: Technology Counts* (March 14, 2013), p. 5.

55 "Wireless Generation," *Education Week: Technology Counts* (March 14, 2013), p. 9.

56 "Amplify Access," *Education Week: Technology Counts* (March 14, 2013), p. 2.

57 Ibid., p. 20.

58 Knewton, "About Knewton." Retrieved from http://www.knewton.com/about/ on March 15, 2013.

59 See Knewton, "The Future of Education Right Now." Retrieved from http://www.knewton.com/pearson/ on March 15, 2013 and Pearson, "MyLab/Mastering." Retrieved from http://pearsonmylabandmastering.com/learn-about/ on March 15, 2013.

60 Education Industry Association, "Mission and Goals." Retrieved from http://www.educationindustry.org/mission-and-goals on March 15, 2013.

61 Education Industry Association, *Mission and Goals*, Retrieved from http://www.educationindustry.org/mission-and-goals on July 9, 2013.

62 Catherine Gewertz, "Educators Questioning Timing of State Tests Reflecting Standards," *Education Week* (March 27, 2013), pp. 1, 14–15.

63 See Core Knowledge Foundation, http://www.coreknowledge.org/.

64 Expeditionary Learning, "Our Approach." Retrieved from http://elschools.org/our-approach on April 1, 2013.

65 Expeditionary Learning, "History." Retrieved from http://elschools.org/about-us/history on April 1, 2013.

66 Gewertz, "Educators Questioning Timing of State Tests Reflecting Standards," p. 14.

67 Public Consulting Group, "About." Retrieved from http://www.publicconsultinggroup.com/about/index.html on April 1, 2013.

68 Miron, et al., *Profiles of For-Profit and Nonprofit Education Management Organizations*, p. i.

69 Ibid., p. ii.
70 Brill, *Class Warfare*, pp. 219–228.
71 Ibid., pp. 236–244 and U. S. Department of Education, "Senior Staff—Arne Duncan, U.S. Secretary of Education—Biography." Retrieved from http://www2.ed.gov/news/staff/bios/duncan.html on March 18, 2013.
72 "Give Children the Best in Education and Watch Their Potential Grow: Ariel Education Initiative, 2007." Brochure retrieved from Ariel Education Initiative http://www.arielinvestments.com/content/view/106/1066/ on December 16, 2008.
73 Ibid.
74 Ibid.
75 Ariel Investments, "Ariel Community Academy." Retrieved from http://www.arielinvestments.com/ariel-community-academy/ on March 18, 2013.
76 Linkedin, "Profile John Petry." Retrieved from http://www.linkedin.com/ on March 19, 2013.
77 Maisie McAdoo, "Attack of the Hedge-fund Managers: Why Do They Care About Schools? It's All About Money," United Federation of Teachers: New York Teacher issue (June 3, 2010). Retrieved from http://www.uft.org/news-stories/attack-hedge-fund-managers on March 19, 2013.
78 Value Investing Congress, "Home." Retrieved from http://www.valueinvestingcongress.com/ on March 19, 2013.
79 Democrats for Education Reform, "Board of Directors." Retrieved from http://www.dfer.org/list/about/board/ on March 19, 2013.
80 Ibid.
81 Brill, *Class Warfare*, pp. 131–132.
82 Ibid., p. 116.
83 Martin Kelly, "Barack Obama – President of the United States." Retrieved from http://americanhistory.about.com/od/biographiesmr/p/barack_obama.htm on March 18, 2013.
84 NYC.gov, "Mayor Michael R. Bloomberg Appoints Joel Klein As Schools Chancellor." Retrieved from http://www.nyc.gov/portal/site/nycgov/menuitem.b270a4a1d51bb3017bce0ed101c789a0/index.jsp?pageID=nyc_blue_room&catID=1194&doc_name=http%3A%2F%2Fwww.nyc.gov%2Fhtml%2Fom%2Fhtml%2F2002b%2Fpr201-02.html&cc=unused1978&rc=1194&ndi=1 on March 22, 2013.
85 Jeremy W. Peters, "Schools Chief Has Much in Common With Boss," *The New York Times* (November 9, 2010). Retrieved from http://www.nytimes.com/2010/11/10/nyregion/10black.html?pagewanted=print on March 22, 2013.
86 Ibid.
87 Ibid.
88 Michael Barbaro, Sharon Otterman, and Javier C. Hernandez, "After 3 Months, Mayor Replaces Schools Leader," *The New York Times* (April 7, 2011). Retrieved from http://www.nytimes.com/2011/04/08/education/08black.html?pagewanted=all on March 22, 2013.
89 Michael Barbaro, "Black Admits Being Ill Prepared," *The New York Times* (April 8, 2011). Retrieved from http://www.nytimes.com/2011/04/09/nyregion/09black.html?pagewanted=print on March 22, 2013.
90 Barbaro, et al., "After 3 Months, Mayor Replaces Schools Leader."
91 Gordon, et al., *Identifying Effective Teachers Using Performance on the Job*.
92 Ibid., p. 5.
93 The Hamilton Project, "Author Robert Gordon." Retrieved from http://www.hamiltonproject.org/about_us/our_people/robert_gordon/ on March 25, 2013.
94 Dartmouth, "Douglas Staiger." Retrieved from http://www.dartmouth.edu/~dstaiger/pub.html on March 25, 2013.

95 Harvard Kennedy School, John F. Kennedy School of Government, "Thomas Kane." Retrieved from http://www.hks.harvard.edu/about/faculty-staff-directory/thomas-kane on March 25, 2013.

96 United States Department of Labor, Bureau of Labor Statistics, "Occupational Outlook Handbook: Projections Overview." Retrieved from http://www.bls.gov/ooh/About/Projections-Overview.htm on March 25, 2013.

97 Ibid.

98 National Association of Home Builders, "Growing Labor Shortages Impeding Housing and Economic Recovery." Retrieved from http://www.nahb.org/news_details.aspx?newsID=15880 on March 25, 2013.

99 United States Department of Labor, Bureau of Labor Statistics, "Occupational Outlook Handbook."

100 Gordon, et al., *Identifying Effective Teachers Using Performance on the Job,* p. 6.

101 Ibid., p. 5.

102 Thomas J. Kane and Douglas O. Staiger, "Using Imperfect Information to Identify Effective Teachers." (April 25, 2005). Unpublished Paper. (Los Angeles: School of Public Affairs, University of California–Los Angeles). Retrieved from https://www.dartmouth.edu/~dstaiger/Papers/2005/Kane%20Staiger%20teacher%20quality%204%2028%2005.pdf on March 26, 2013.

103 Ibid.

104 Ibid.

105 Ibid.

106 Gordon, et al., *Identifying Effective Teachers Using Performance on the Job,* p. 6.

107 The New Teacher Project, "Teacher Evaluation 2.0 (2010)." Retrieved from http://tntp.org/assets/documents/Teacher-Evaluation-Oct10F.pdf?files/Teacher-Evaluation-Oct10F.pdf on March 27, 2013.

108 Ibid.

109 David L. Kirp, "Making Schools Work," *The New York Times* (May 19, 2012). Retrieved from http://www.nytimes.com/2012/05/20/opinion/sunday/integration-worked-why-have-we-rejected-it.html?_r=0 on March 27, 2013.

110 Gary Orfield, John Kucsera, and Genevieve Siegel-Hawley, "E Pluribus . . . Deepening Double Segregation for More Students," UCLA Civil Rights Project (September 2012). Retrieved from http://civilrightsproject.ucla.edu/research/k-12-education/integration-and-diversity/mlk-national/e-pluribus . . . separation-deepening-double-segregation-for-more-students on March 27, 2013.

111 Ibid., p. 7.

112 Ibid., p. 9.

113 Ibid., pp. 7–8.

114 Ibid., p. 77.

115 Ibid., pp. 79–80.

116 Wendy Kopp, *One Day, All Children . . . The Unlikely Triumph of Teach for America and What I Learned Along the Way* (New York: PublicAffairs, 2011), p. 6.

117 Ibid., p. 7.

118 Ibid., p. 20.

119 Ibid., p. 21.

120 Ibid., pp. 52–54.

121 Ibid., p. 52.

122 Ibid., p. 52.

123 Michelle Rhee, *Radical: Fighting to Put Students First* (New York: HarperCollins, 2013), p. 35.

124 Ibid., pp. 38–39.

125 Ibid., p. 41.

126 Ibid., p. 35.

127 Ibid., p. 53.

128 Ibid., pp. 67–75.

129 Ibid., p. 81.

130 Ibid., p. 286.

131 Ibid., p. 286.

132 StudentsFirst, "About." Retrieved from http://www.studentsfirst.org/pages/about-students-first on March 29, 2013.

133 StudentsFirst, "Board of Directors." Retrieved from http://www.studentsfirst.org/pages/studentsfirst-board-of-directors on March 29, 2013.

134 StudentsFirst, "Policy Agenda," p. 3. Retrieved from http://www.studentsfirst.org/page/-/StudentsFirst_Policy_Agenda.pdf?nocdn=1 on March 25. 2013.

135 KIPP, "About." Retrieved from http://www.kipp.org/about-kipp/history on April 1, 2013.

136 Miron, et al., *Profiles of For-Profit and Nonprofit Education Management Organizations*, p. iii.

3

THE REPUBLICAN PARTY, RACE TO THE TOP, AND CHOICE

In April, 2013, the Republican National Committee (RNC) passed a resolution that rejected the Common Core State Standards and the inBloom database:

> RESOLVED, the Republican National Committee recognizes the CCSS [Common Core State Curriculum] for what it is – an inappropriate overreach to standardize and control the education of our children so they will conform to a preconceived "normal."
>
> RESOLVED, That the Republican National Committee rejects the collection of personal student data for any non-educational purpose without the prior written consent of an adult student or a child student's parent and that it rejects the sharing of such personal data, without the prior written consent of an adult student or a child student's parent, with any person or entity other than schools or education agencies within the state.[1]

On the surface this seemed to contradict, as I will explain in more detail later in the chapter, a Republican commitment to curriculum standards beginning with President George H. W. Bush's administration (1988–1992). This change was foreshadowed in the 2012 election when the Republican criticized federal intervention in public schools and returned to its continuing theme of school choice.

The conservative Thomas B. Fordham Institute, which supported the Common Core State Standards, posted this on its website after the resolution was approved:

> Count us among those surprised and alarmed by the Republican National Committee's ill-considered decision to adopt a **resolution** decrying the Common Core standards as a "nationwide straitjacket on

academic freedom and achievement." There's little doubt that this action will bestow a degree of legitimacy upon the anti-standards coalition—and put pressure on Republican governors and legislators to fall in line.[2]

I will begin this chapter by analyzing the Republican resolution against the Common Core State Standards and how it reflects education sections of the 2012 Republican Party platform. This will be followed by a discussion of Republican commitment to educational choice and standards.

RNC Resolution on the Common Core State Standards and the 2012 Republican Platform

The wording of the RNC's 2013 resolution on the Common Core State Standards parallels the wording used in the 2012 Republican platform and reflects the traditional commitment of the Party to school choice. The resolution opens:

> WHEREAS, the Common Core State Standards (CCSS) are a set of academic standards ... [is] a method for conforming American students to uniform ("one size fits all") achievement goals to make them more competitive in a global marketplace.[3]

The 2012 Republican platform states: "We do not believe in a one size fits all approach to education and support providing broad education choices to parents and children at the State and local level."[4] The 2012 Republican platform also backs away from the commitment, as I explain later in this chapter, to Republican President George W. Bush's support and implementation of the 2001 legislation No Child Left Behind. However, while backing away from federal involvement, the platform does continue to stress the importance of accountability. The 2012 Republican platform refers to the centralizing of reform efforts as a disaster in the context of expanding school choice:

> Education is much more than schooling. It is the whole range of activities by which families and communities transmit to a younger generation, not just knowledge and skills, but ethical and behavioral norms and traditions. It is the handing over of a personal and cultural identity. That is why education choice has expanded so vigorously. It is also why *American education has, for the last several decades, been the focus of constant controversy, as centralizing forces outside the family and community have sought to remake education in order to remake America. They have not succeeded, but they have done immense damage* [author's emphasis].[5]

The 2013 RNC resolution complains about the use of outside money, such as the Bill and Melinda Gates Foundation, to create the Common Core State

Standards. The resolution claims the creation of the Common Core State Standards violated freedom of information and sunshine laws. Most importantly, the resolution complains about the lack of piloting the Common Core State Standards before states implemented them. As I stressed in Chapters 1 and 2, there was no longitudinal research about the effect of the Common Core State Standards on student learning or preparation for college or the global workforce. The RNC resolution states:

> WHEREAS, the NGA [National Governors Association] and the CCSSO [Council of Chief State School Officers], received tens of millions of dollars from private third parties to advocate for and develop the CCSS [Common Core State Standards] strategy, subsequently created the CCSS through a process that was not subject to any freedom of information acts or other sunshine laws, and never piloted the CCSS.[6]

Besides complaining that the Common Core State Standards were never piloted, the resolution argues that because of federal pressure "they failed to give states, their legislatures and their citizen's time to evaluate the CCSS."[7] The resolution claims that the federal actions resulted in violating a prohibition against creating a national curriculum: "WHEREAS, even though Federal Law prohibits the federalizing of curriculum, the Obama Administration accepted the CCSS plan and used 2009 Stimulus Bill money to reward the states that were most committed to the president's CCSS agenda."[8]

Surprisingly, for those who think of Republicans as always supporting business interests, the resolution criticized the close association between test makers and the products being sold to fulfill the requirements of the Common Core State Standards:

> WHEREAS, the NGA and CCSSO in concert with the same *corporations developing the CCSS "assessments" have created new textbooks, digital media and other teaching materials aligned to the standards* which must be purchased and adopted by local school districts in order that students may effectively compete on CCSS "assessments" [author's emphasis].[9]

Not surprisingly, given traditional Republican concerns about personal liberty, the RNC criticized inBloom for its national collection of student data. It proposed that any action of this sort required parental consent to both the collection of student data and its sharing with "entities" other than education agencies. And, as I will elaborate in the next section, the RNC considered the Common Core State Standards as a threat to real choice in education.

Republicans and School Choice

Since the 1980s, the Republican Party has supported school choice plans. More recently, the RNC's resolution on the Common Core State Standards, the 2012 Republican platform, and the actions of Republican governors have reinforced the goal of parental choice of schools, including the use of vouchers and tax credits to choose private schools. At the same time, Republicans support accountability of schools by states and local school districts. As I will explain later in this section, the Republican Party's official position is that choice creates market competition between competing types of curricula, methods of instruction, and school organization.

For instance, the RNC rejects the Common Core State Standards because they limit choice in education. In other words, the Common Core State Standards require the use of assessments based on its standards. Teachers must teach for the tests based on the Common Core State Standards. This has a determining effect on a school's curricula and classroom teaching. The RNC's resolution states:

> *WHEREAS*, the CCSS effectively *removes educational choice and competition* since all schools and all districts must use Common Core "assessments" based on the Common Core standards to allow all students to advance in the school system and to advance to higher education pursuits [author's emphasis].[10]

In this context, the writers of the RNC's resolution consider choice more than just parents choosing between schools that they think better implements the Common Core State Standards. Real choice, from this perspective, is between schools with differing curricula and methods of instruction. The 2012 Republican platform has this statement on school choice: "Today's education reform ... recognizes the wisdom of State and local control of our schools, and it wisely sees *consumer rights in education—choice—as the most important driving force for renewing our schools* [author's emphasis]."[11] The platform does stress the importance of accountability and high expectations, but does not mention curriculum standards: "Today's education reform movement calls for accountability at every stage of schooling. It affirms higher expectations for all students and rejects the crippling bigotry of low expectations."[12]

Some Republican-controlled states initiated school choice programs that carry out the national platform. In 2012, Louisiana's Republican Governor Bobby Jindal championed an expansion of the 2008 voucher program to include private and religious schools. The state's legislature passed the law which was also supported, according to *The Times-Picayune* reporter Lauren McGaughy, by "the pro-school choice group the Louisiana Black Alliance for Educational Options, [because] it allows parents more control over their child's education by providing a wider list of school options."[13] In March 2013, the Indiana Supreme Court ruled that the state's voucher plan, which parents can use at private schools, was constitutional. This plan, according to Reuters' reporter Stephanie Simon:

> is considered the broadest in the United States because it is not limited to low-income students or those attending failing schools – and because it is available to children statewide. A family of four with a household income of $64,000 a year is eligible for vouchers worth up to $4,500 per child.[14]

On January 1, 2013 Arizona's new voucher plan went into effect with the support of a predominantly Republican state legislature and a Republican governor. Writing in *The Republic*, reporter Anne Ryman describes the program: "One out of every five Arizona students in public schools becomes eligible today to apply for public money to attend private schools this fall under an expansion of a controversial voucher-type program."[15] The vouchers are received in the form of a debit card that can be used at private schools.

The above are examples of Republican-dominated state governments that reflect both the RNC's statement on the Common Core State Standards and the issue of choice in the 2012 Republican platform. This is consistent with Republican positions in the past and is based, in part, on theories about the workings of free markets and school choice which can be traced to the work of Friedrich Hayek, an Austrian economist and Nobel Prize winner, who moved to the U.S. to teach at the University of Chicago from 1950 to 1962.

Republicans and Free Market Theory

Friedrich Hayek influenced a number of American economists, including Murray Rothbard, William Simon, and Milton Friedman. In their most radical anarcholibertarian form, Austrian economists such as Rothbard advocated abolishing all forms of government and applying free-market theory to every aspect of living, including highways, law enforcement, defense, and schooling.[16] Without government interference, these Austrian economists argued, marketplace competition would create ideal institutions. Applied to schooling, this meant no government provision or control of education. Instead, entrepreneurs would organize schools and compete for students while the "invisible hand" of the marketplace determined what forms of schooling were best.

Hayek's economic ideas played a major role in the Reagan–style Republicanism of the 1980s and 1990s and in conservative attacks on liberalism and government bureaucracy. In the 1930s, Hayek debated English economist John Maynard Keynes over the role of government in a capitalist system. Keynes argued that for capitalism to survive, governments needed to intervene in the economy. Classical liberals, such as John Stuart Mill, opposed government intervention, but the progressive liberals of the 1930s justified government intervention to ensure equality of opportunity and provide a social safety net as necessary for the survival of capitalism.[17]

In *The Road to Serfdom*, Hayek set the stage for later conservative criticisms of government bureaucracies, including educational bureaucracies. He argued that the difficulty of determining prices or the value of goods would inevitably cause the failure of centrally planned economies. According to Hayek, pricing determines the social value of goods: What should a car cost in relation to food? What should the price of health care be in relation to education? In a free market, Hayek asserted, prices or social values are determined by individual choice. In a planned economy, pricing or social value is determined by a government bureaucracy. What criterion is used by a government bureaucracy? Hayek's answer was that the inevitable criterion is one that promotes the personal advantage of bureaucracy members. Bureaucrats and intellectuals supported by a bureaucracy, he argued, will advance social theories that vindicate the continued existence and expansion of the bureaucracy.[18]

Defining the enemy as the bureaucracy is one of Hayek's enduring legacies. Many educational critics complain that the problem with public schools is the educational bureaucracy. A frequently heard statement regarding schools is: "The problem is not money! The problem is bureaucratic waste!" By placing the blame on the educational bureaucracy, school reformers can avoid the issue of equal funding among school districts. Some public school students receive the benefits of living in well-financed suburban school districts, whereas others languish in overcrowded classrooms in poorly funded school districts that lack adequate textbooks and educational materials. Blaming the bureaucracy became an easy method for avoiding increased educational funding.

Beginning in the 1950s and lasting into the 21st century, Republicans claimed that a major problem is control of schools by a self-serving educational bureaucracy. In addition, as discussed in Chapter 4, right-wing Republicans insist that the liberal elite controls the culture of universities, public schools, and the media. Hayek identified these liberal elite as a new class composed of government experts and their intellectual supporters. Within this framework schools could improve only if the power of the educational bureaucrats was broken and schools functioned according to the dictates of market competition.

Friedman, a colleague of Hayek's at the University of Chicago and 1976 Nobel Prize winner, became the first American, at least to my knowledge, to advocate the use of vouchers as a means of providing school choice. In contrast to Rothbard, Friedman argued that the benefits of maintaining a stable and democratic society justified government support of education, but not government-operated schools. Friedman proposed a government-financed voucher that parents could redeem "for a specified maximum sum per child per years if spent on 'approved' educational services."[19] Friedman believed the resulting competition between private schools for government vouchers would improve the quality of education.

Also, Friedman contended in the 1960s that vouchers would overcome the class stratification that results from the existence of rich and poor school districts. Friedman suggested, "Under present arrangements, stratification of residential areas effectively restricts the intermingling of children from decidedly different backgrounds."[20] Except for a few parochial schools, Friedman argued, private schools were too expensive for most families, which resulted in further social class divisions in education.

Like Friedman, many Republicans embraced the concept of the free market but rejected the idea of completely abandoning government control, particularly social and moral control. After the riots and student rebellions of the 1960s and 1970s, Republicans believed that the government should exercise moral authority over social life. Free market ideologists contended that competition in the education market will result in improving the quality of education available to the American public. An unusual aspect of this argument is the support given to for-profit education. It is argued that a for-profit school will be more attuned to balancing costs with quality school instruction while trying to please parents. A for-profit education institution will want to market a good product to attract customers and control costs to ensure a profit.

Republicans were able to get their ideas on for-profit education into No Child Left Behind. Scattered throughout No Child Left Behind are provisions to support for-profit companies. For instance, the legislation states that assistance to schools requiring improvement because of low test scores can be provided by a "for–profit agency."[21] Under the Reading First section, reading and literacy partnerships can be established between school districts and for-profit companies.[22] Also, state and local school districts are provided funds to contract with for-profit companies to provide advanced placement courses and services to reform teacher and principal certification; to recruit "highly qualified teachers, including specialists in core academic subjects, principals, and pupil services personnel"; "to improve science and mathematics curriculum and instruction"; "to develop State and local teacher corps or other programs to establish, expand, and enhance teacher recruitment and retention efforts"; to integrate "proven teaching practices into instruction"; for professional development programs; to provide services to teachers of limited English proficient students and for developing and implementing programs for limited English proficient students; to create and expand community technology centers; to accredit basic education of Indian children in Bureau of Indian Affairs schools; and to train prospective teachers in advanced technology.[23]

The development of for-profit schools was closely tied to the development of charter schools. Educational entrepreneur Chris Whittle came up with the idea of franchising for-profit schools. Whittle was counting on a government voucher system that would allow parents to choose between private and public schools. Whittle wanted to capture some of this voucher money by designing a conservative and technologically advanced school that could be franchised across the country.

Politically, Whittle is a Republican. He made his position in the culture wars evident when he convinced the Federal Express Corporation to help fund the publication of Schlesinger's attack on multicultural education, *The Disuniting of America.*[24] Schlesinger's book carries the imprint of Whittle Direct Books and has full-page ads for Federal Express scattered through the text. Whittle tried to ensure that Schlesinger's educational ideas received a wide audience by sending free copies to business leaders around the country.

Whittle's political views are exemplified by his selection of the conservative President of Yale University, Benno Schmidt, to head his for-profit school enterprise. Whittle made the decision to hire Schmidt over food and drinks at a party in the ultra-exclusive Hamptons on Long Island. Offered an annual salary of about $1 million, Schmidt left Yale in 1992 to head what was called the Edison Project. As one of the consultants on the project, Whittle hired Chester Finn, an important Republican educator who I will discuss later in this chapter.[25]

Part of Whittle's plans went awry when the 1992 election of President Clinton seemed to doom any chance of government-financed public–private school vouchers.[26] Without public–private school vouchers, the only hope for the Edison Project was to franchise private schools that were dependent on tuition income or to seek some other form of public support. The opportunity for public support came, according to *New York Magazine* reporter James Traub, when:

> governors William Weld of Massachusetts and Buddy Roemer of Colorado contacted Schmidt in the fall of 1992 that they would like to find a way to bring Edison into the public schools in their states. Both states went on to pass "charter school" laws that permit states and school systems to award contracts to . . . private contractors.[27]

With charter schools, the operation of for-profit schools became a possibility.

Edison schools are an example of a leading for-profit education company. In 2008, the company was renamed EdisonLearning after it acquired another for-profit software company. This acquisition is described in a corporate announcement:

> In 2008, a major company transformation took place with the . . . acquisition of the education software company Provost Systems, Edison Learning combines its experience and core competencies in teaching and learning with a fully integrated online and Web-based technology solution that can dramatically achieve universal student access to a genuine, individualized learning experience.[28]

In 2013, EdisonLearning acknowledged its pioneering role in developing charter schools and its global reach.

> Edison Learning is a leading international educational solutions provider
> with nearly 20 years of experience partnering with schools, districts,
> governments, organizations, charter authorizers, and boards. We *pioneered*
> *the concept of charter schools in the U.S.* ... Since our founding, Edison Learning
> has educated more than one million students, and currently serves partners
> with more than 450,000 students in 25 states, the United Kingdom and the
> Middle East through 391 school partnerships [author's emphasis].[29]

The problem for Republicans was convincing the public, politicians, and
educators that the public school monopoly resulted in low-quality schooling. Free
markets and competition, they claimed, would lift educational quality to new
heights. As described in the following sections, selling the idea of free markets
in education would occur through the influence of conservative think tanks,
foundations, and Christian organizations.

Planning an Educational Revolution: The Trickle-Down Theory of Ideas and No Child Left Behind

Selling the public on vouchers and free markets, and eventually academic standards
and testing, was the result of conscious efforts by conservative private foundations to recruit scholars and disseminate their agendas for education. Their efforts
paid off with the passage of No Child Left Behind. My first realization of this
attempt to revolutionize education occurred in the early 1970s, at a meeting
at the Institute for Humane Studies in Menlo Park, California. Discussion at
the meeting focused on how to organize a cadre of intellectuals to openly support
freedom and capitalism because colleges and universities were hopelessly controlled by left-wing intellectuals. I was one of those academics, they hoped, who
could be persuaded to spread conservative ideas into academic establishments
and to policymakers. Being elitists, these conservatives wanted to focus their
efforts on intellectual and political leaders. Just as supply-side economists
would later talk about trickle-down economics, these conservatives believed in
trickle-down ideas.

At the time, I did not understand this to be part of a movement later
described by James Smith in his 1991 book, *The Idea Brokers and the Rise of the*
New Policy Elite: "In the early 1970s, executives in a handful of traditionally
conservative foundations redefined their programs with the aim of shaping the
public policy agenda and constructing a network of conservative institutions
and scholars."[30] One of the leaders and articulate spokespersons of this movement was William Simon, who left his job in 1976 as Secretary of the Treasury
in the Nixon and Ford administrations to become head of the John M.
Olin Foundation, the purpose of which, in Simon's words, "is to support
those individuals and institutions who are working to strengthen the free
enterprise system."[31]

Reflecting Simon's economic beliefs, the preface and foreword for his book *A Time for Truth* were written, respectively, by Friedman and Hayek. In the preface, Friedman sounded the warning that intellectual life in the U.S. was under the control of "socialists and interventionists, who have wrongfully appropriated in this country the noble label 'liberal' and who have been the intellectual architects of our suicidal course."[32] Applying concepts of the marketplace to intellectual life, Friedman argued that the payoff for these "liberals" was support by an entrenched government bureaucracy. In other words, the liberal elite and the government bureaucracy fed off each other. Using a phrase that would be repeated by conservatives throughout the rest of the 20th century, Friedman contended that "the view that government is the problem, not the cure," is hard for the public to understand.[33] According to Friedman's plea, saving the country required a group of intellectuals to promote a general understanding of the importance of the free market.

To undermine the supposed rule of a liberal intelligentsia, Simon urged the business community to support intellectuals who advocated the importance of the free market. Simon called on businesspeople to stop supporting colleges and universities that produced "young collectivists by the thousands" and media "which serve as megaphones for anticapitalist opinion." In both cases, Simon insisted, businesspeople should focus their support on university programs and media that stress procapitalist ideas.[34]

In his call for action, Simon calculated that the first step should involve businesspeople rushing "multimillions to the aid of liberty, in the many places where it is beleaguered." On receiving the largesse of business, he insisted, "Foundations imbued with the philosophy of freedom ... must take pains to funnel desperately needed funds to scholars, social scientists, writers, and journalists who understand the relationship between political and economic liberty."[35]

In light of Simon's leadership of the John M. Olin Foundation in the 1970s, it is interesting that two of the leading writers for the conservative cause in education, Chester Finn, Jr. and Dinesh D'Souza, are, respectively, John M. Olin Fellow at the Manhattan Institute and the American Enterprise Institute (AEI). Besides supporting scholars at the conservative Manhattan Institute and the AEI, the John M. Olin Foundation backed many right-wing causes and, according to one writer, "its pattern of giving became [in the 1970s] more sophisticated and more closely attuned to the potential of grantees for influencing debates on national politics."[36]

Although conservatives talk about the invisible hand of the free market, the trickle-down distribution of ideas has been very well planned with the following methods being used:

1. Creating foundations and institutes that fund research and policy statements supportive of school choice, privatization of public schools, and, more recently, charter schools.

2. Identifying scholars to conduct research, write policy statements, and lecture at public forums that are favorable to school choice, privatization of public schools, and charter schools.
3. Financing conferences to bring like-minded scholars together for the sharing of ideas and the creation of edited books.
4. Paying scholars to write newspaper opinion pieces that are then distributed to hundreds of newspapers across the country.

This fourth point is an important element in the trickle-down theory of ideas. It is a big leap from writing a research report to being featured on the opinion-editorial page of *The New York Times* or other leading newspapers. This frequently occurs with conservatively-backed educational commentators, such as Chester Finn, Jr. and Diane Ravitch. It requires connections and a public relations staff to gain quick access to the media. Providing this type of access is one of the important elements in the strategy for spreading the conservative agenda. With public relations help from conservatives, I appeared in the 1970s as an "academic expert" on radio and television shows across the country. On one occasion, after the physical exercise portion of an early morning television show, I fielded call-in questions ranging from "Why can't my daughter read?" to "Why are all college professors socialists?" There was never any hint that my appearance on the program resulted from the work of conservative organizations.

In *The Transformation of American Politics*, David Ricci described the attempt to mobilize and control public opinion. "Those who talked about developing conservative ideas," Ricci stated, "were committed not just to producing them but to the commercial concept of a product, in the sense of something that, once created, must be placed before the public as effectively as possible."[37]

The Heritage Foundation and the AEI: Marketing School Reform

The Heritage Foundation and the AEI are the two largest conservative think tanks. They play major roles in shaping the Republican Party's education agenda. Both think tanks fund policy development and disseminate polices and reports to politicians, other policymakers, and the general public. They cover a broad range of policy issues from national defense to education. The overwhelming majority of scholars funded by these organizations are considered politically conservative.

In 2013, The Heritage Foundation described itself:

> The Heritage Foundation is a unique institution-a public policy research organization, or "think tank". We draw solutions to contemporary problems from the ideas, principles and traditions that make America great.

We are not afraid to begin our sentences with the words "We believe," because we do believe: in individual liberty, free enterprise, limited government, a strong national defense, and traditional American values.[38]

Reflecting its intellectual debt to Friedrich Hayek, The Heritage Foundation offered to new members a free copy of Hayek's *Road to Serfdom*.[39]

One of the organizers of The Heritage Foundation, Edwin Fuelner, referred to it as a "secondhand dealer in ideas."[40] The Heritage Foundation developed out of a plan by Pat Buchanan at the request of Republican President Richard Nixon. Shortly after Nixon's 1972 election, Buchanan proposed the creation of an institute that would be a repository of Republican beliefs and would provide a Republican talent bank for conservative thinkers. Buchanan, along with Fuelner and Paul Weyrich, solicited $250,000 in financial support from Joseph Coors, the Colorado brewer and supporter of conservative causes. Opening its doors in 1973, The Heritage Foundation received further support from the John M. Olin Foundation and John Scaife, a Mellon heir and another supporter of conservative causes.[41] After the 1980 election, The Heritage Foundation presented President Reagan's White House transition team with a 1,000-page volume entitled *Mandate for Change*. The volume, which summarized Republican thinking about a broad range of issues, including education, set the tone and direction of the Reagan administration.

Called the General Motors of conservative think tanks, The Heritage Foundation published Chester Finn, Jr. and Diane Ravitch's 1995 report on school reform in their monthly *Policy Review*. In the same issue appeared an article by Dinesh D'Souza, who at the time was the John M. Olin scholar at the AEI.[42] As described earlier in this book, D'Souza's article, "We the Slaveowners: In Jefferson's America, Were Some Men Not Created Equal?" provided an upbeat note to American slavery.[43]

In 2013, The Heritage Foundation continued to oppose federal involvement in school policies. For example, it released a policy statement criticizing President Barack Obama's call for universal preschool:

> In February 2013, President Obama proposed significantly increasing federal spending on early childhood education and care as part of his drive for a "cradle-to-career" government-controlled education system. A massive federal preschool expansion would further entangle Washington in the education and care of the youngest American children … The evidence from other preschool programs also indicates that the potential benefits of universal preschool may be overstated.[44]

Reflecting its debt to Friedrich Hayek and its support of school choice plans by the Republican Party, The Heritage Foundation posted on its 2013 website: "Whether through education savings accounts, tax credit scholarship programs, vouchers, online learning, charter schools, or homeschooling, school choice allows access to quality education options that best match individual children's learning needs."[45] Reflecting a free-market ideology, The Heritage Foundation claimed:

> School choice options place competitive pressure on public school systems to improve and meet the needs of students. When families have options, public schools must meet the needs of children or risk losing enrollments—and hence dollars—creating a strong incentive for improvement.[46]

It listed what it thought were the benefits of school choice:

1. Leads to improved academic outcomes.
2. Significantly increases graduation rates.
3. Increases student safety.
4. Improves parental satisfaction with their child's academic and social development and satisfaction with their child's school overall.
5. Introduces competitive pressure on the public education system that lifts all boats, improving outcomes for students who exercise school choice as well as students who remain in public schools.
6. And, most importantly, allows parents to access educational options that meet their child's unique learning needs.[47]

Reflecting the religious right's influence on The Heritage Foundation, Matthew Spalding at the 25th Annual Resource Bank Meeting of The Heritage Foundation, restated the argument that religion was the basis of American society:

> Republican government was possible only if the private virtues needed for civil society and self-government remained strong and effective. The civic responsibility and moderation of public passion also requires the moderation of private passion through the encouragement of individual morality. And the best way to encourage morality is through the flourishing of religion and the establishment of traditional moral habits.[48]

He went on to state that the lack of government support of morality was the chief cause of American problems:

> There is a deeper problem as well. Not only does progressive liberalism deny a substantive role for morality in public life, but the extended reach of the state has forced traditional morality—the ground of the old idea of character—into a smaller and smaller private sphere. The sharp distinction between public and private, accompanied by the expansion of the governmental sphere, points toward the privatization of morality. If all

values are relative, and freedom now means liberation of the human will, it is hard to see any restraints on individual choice. The effect that this combination of things has had on education, religion, and the family— with the rise of illegitimacy and the breakdown of marriage—has been devastating.[49]

In contrast to the dissemination role of The Heritage Foundation, the AEI focuses on supporting Republican scholarship. Originally organized in 1943 to educate the public about business, the AEI dramatically changed in the 1960s under the leadership of William J. Baroody, who applied the concepts of Austrian economics to the world of ideas. Baroody believed there existed a liberal monopoly of ideas. Baroody argued that "a free society can tolerate some degree of concentration in the manufacture of widgets. But the day it approaches a monopoly in idea formation, that is its death knell."[50]

Baroody proposed a free market of ideas by breaking the liberal monopoly through the establishment of conservative think tanks. Once competition was created, he believed, the invisible hand of the marketplace would determine the value of particular ideas. During the early 1970s, Melvin Laird, Secretary of Defense in the Republican Nixon administration, kicked off a $25 million fund-raising campaign for the AEI in a Pentagon dining room. By the 1980s, the Institute had a staff of 150 and an annual budget of more than $10 million.

In 2013, on its page for Policy Studies, the AEI warned about the Common Core State Standards: "If the Common Core is pursued with insufficient thought to practical and policy implications, the movement is at risk of stifling the next generation of instruction and assessment, as well as other education reforms."[51] Like The Heritage Foundation, the AEI continues to support school choice and vouchers. In a posted policy study, it claims:

> A survey of the research literature on private school voucher programs shows a consistent pattern. School voucher programs are associated with positive (though small) results for participating students and positive (but also small) results for those students that remain in traditional public schools.[52]

While criticizing the Common Core State Standards, both The Heritage Foundation and the AEI supported No Child Left Behind. On September 4, 2004, The Heritage Foundation issued educational guidelines to parents praising No Child Left Behind because it provided information on student scores to parents and its limited support of school choice:

> As the summer winds down, children everywhere race to finish their summer reading assignments and parents begin their search for new notebooks, bigger backpacks, and maybe even better schools.

Two years after the enactment of the No Child Left Behind Act parents have access to more information about the quality of public schools than ever before. No Child Left Behind's reporting requirements make schools more accountable to parents. Schools must issue certain specific information about achievement in reading and math, and schools that persistently fail to educate children at grade level must offer new options, such as tutoring and school choice. Armed with information and empowered by this new authority, parents are in a better position than ever before to choose where their children attend school.[53]

Eleven days after The Heritage Foundation issued its 2004 parental guide, the AEI hosted a conference on No Child Left Behind where Frederick Hess, director of education policy at the AEI and Chester Finn of the Thomas B. Fordham Institute, offered their analysis of the legislation.[54] At the meeting, Finn primarily complained about the legislation not completely carrying out the Republican education agenda and that the legislation required some internal tinkering. The choice options supported by No Child Left Behind were considered by Finn to be lagging:

The supply of high-achieving schools, alternative options, and support programs do not keep up with the demand for choice provided by NCLB [No Child Left Behind]. More creative options need to be explored, including charter schools, home schools, cyber-schools, private schools, and inter-district transfers.[55]

Hess contended that:

NCLB is today too lenient about the skills and knowledge that students must acquire and too prescriptive about calendars, state improvement targets, and school sanctions. We suggest that there is a reasonable level of nationwide agreement as to what children should learn in reading and mathematics. Federal lawmakers should take advantage of that consensus.[56]

In 2007, as part of No Child Left Behind's reauthorization, The Heritage Foundation gave its support to federal legislation titled "Academic Partnerships Lead Us to Success (A-PLUS) Act" sponsored by Republican Senators Jim DeMint of South Carolina and John Cornyn of Texas and Republican Representative Pete Hoekstra of Michigan. While supporting the basic tenets of No Child Left Behind, Heritage Foundation officials were concerned about its extension of federal power over local schools. This has been a major dilemma for conservatives who on the one hand called for limiting and reducing federal power and on the other hand supported one of the greatest invasions of federal power in local education. According to The Heritage Foundation, both the Senate and House forms of the "A–PLUS Act . . . promote greater state and local control in education while maintaining true accountability through state-level testing and information reporting to parents to ensure transparency."[57]

The Heritage Foundation continued to market its educational ideas. In 2007, the organization published *A Parent's Guide to Education Reform*.[58] The goal of the guide was increasing parental control of education through school choice which in this case includes choice of public, private sectarian, and religious schools. The guide's major sections are devoted to school choice, including "Why America's Parents Need Greater Choice in Education," "School Choice: A Growing Option in American Education,""Private School Choice," and "Other Forms of School Choice."[59]

In response to President Obama's Race to the Top, the AEI sponsored an April 6, 2009 conference titled: "Race to the Top? The Promise—and—Challenges of Charter School Growth."[60] The conference was in response to President Obama's efforts to provide more money for charter schools. Headlining the conference was AEI scholar Frederick Hess. Staging a conference to disseminate the ideas of the Institute is a favorite marketing tactic, which in this case meant marketing ideas about charter schools.[61]

The Manhattan Institute and the Republican Agenda

The Manhattan's slogan is "Turning Intellect Into Influence" and its stated mission "is to develop and disseminate new ideas that foster greater economic choice and individual responsibility."[62]

> Similar to the Republican Party, the Manhattan Institute promotes choice and vouchers: Expansive school choice in the form of vouchers and charter schools is the most attractive option available for improving urban schools. A wide body of evidence accumulated over the last decade shows that school choice helps kids, increases the effectiveness of public schools, and saves taxpayer dollars.[63]

The Manhattan Institute also supports charter schools as an option for children from low-income families:

> Charter schools can dramatically improve the education provided to a city's students. For instance, Stanford University economist Caroline Hoxby found that students attending charter schools in New York City performed much better in both math and reading than they would have had they remained in the public schools. The KIPP charter school network, which currently operates charter schools in nineteen states and the District of Columbia, has had phenomenal success improving student proficiency and sending overwhelmingly low-income students to college.[64]

During the Republican administration of George W. Bush, the Manhattan Institute proudly listed on its website its influence on Bush. First on the list were two supporters of compassionate conservatism as preached by Marvin Olasky and supported by the Institute. The Manhattan Institute's John Dilulio was appointed Director of the White House Office of Faith-Based and Community Initiatives, and Stephen Goldsmith was named Special Advisor to the President for Faith-Based and Community Initiatives. Influence on economic policy was assured by the Institute's former Senior Fellow Lawrence Lindsay acting as Chief Economic Advisor to Bush and the appointment of the Institute's David Frum as Special Assistant to the President for Economic Speech Writing. While at the Institute, Lindsay wrote the book that influenced Bush's tax policies: *The Growth Experiment: How the New Tax Policy Is Transforming the U.S. Economy*. The Institute's influence on civil rights issues was assured by the appointment of Senior Fellow Abigail Thernstrom to the U.S. Commission on Civil Rights. Also, the Institute cited Senior Fellow Myron Magnet's book, *The Dream and the Nightmare*, as "The book that helped shape Bush's message."[65]

The Manhattan Institute devotes a great amount of attention to school choice and testing. At the Center for Civic Innovation of the Manhattan Institute, Jay Greene works as Senior Fellow in the field of education and heads the Manhattan Institute's Florida-based Education Research Office. According to the 2004 Manhattan Institute's website, Jay Greene's work on education reform focuses on improving two main reforms of public education: school choice and accountability. School choice reforms (including charter schools and school vouchers) are dedicated to improving the options available to parents of children in public schools and making public schools more directly accountable to parents for education outcomes. Accountability reforms are devoted to improving educational achievement by focusing on imparting knowledge and skills and making teachers, administrators, and students accountable for success or failure.[66]

The Manhattan Institute's influence on national educational policies involves an amalgamation of politics and think tank intellectuals. The Manhattan Institute is a nonprofit organization that funds scholarly work for the purpose of influencing public policy. "The Manhattan Institute," the opening line posted on its website declares, "has been an important force in shaping American political culture."[67] This is followed by the statement "We have supported and publicized research on our era's most challenging public policy issues: taxes, welfare, crime, the legal system, urban life, race, education, and many other topics."[68]

Even more revealing of its open use of scholarship to promote certain political and educational causes is the statement accompanying its plea for donations. Written by the Institute's trustee, Walter Wriston, the contribution form states:

> The Institute's intellectual capital far exceeds its financial capital, making it the most cost-effective organization of its kind. Although the impact of our ideas dwarfs our financial resources, we still need the latter. There is not a better bargain to be had.[69]

Educational policy was George W. Bush's topic when he spoke at the Manhattan Institute during the 2000 primary campaign. At the Institute, Bush was warmly greeted as "my homeboy" by former congressman Reverend Floyd Flake.[70] In this tangled web of connections, Flake had, just before introducing Bush, accepted the headship of the charter school division of the Edison Schools Inc., the largest for-profit school-management company in the country. Flake is listed on the "Education Reform" section of the Manhattan Institute's website along with former U.S. Department of Education Assistant Secretaries Chester E. Finn, Jr. and Diane Ravitch as being "at the forefront of today's thinking about how our children's educational achievement can be increased."[71]

Bush's proposal to give vouchers to parents of children in failing schools closely parallels the policies promoted by the Manhattan Institute. Bush and Republican leaders contemplated that parents whose children were in schools that consistently had failing test scores would be given the choice of using federal Title I funds to send their children to private schools. This plan would eventually become part of No Child Left Behind. The plan was similar to the one praised in the Manhattan Institute's publication on Florida's A-Plus accountability and school choice program, operated under the leadership of George W. Bush's brother, Florida's Republican Governor Jeb Bush. The Institute's report, authored by Jay P. Greene, claimed that:

> By offering vouchers to students at failing schools, the Florida A-Plus choice and accountability system was intended to motivate those schools to improve ... This report found that students' academic test scores improve when public schools are faced with the prospect that their students will receive vouchers.[72]

Vouchers are a target area on the Manhattan Institute's education agenda. With the objective of influencing public debate, the Institute's official program description states that "Educational reform is the top public policy concern today, so it should come as no surprise that the Manhattan Institute has the best education reform experts in the country to offer practical advice to policymakers."[73] Also, as part of its research agenda, the Institute is focusing on vouchers as a method for helping low-income parents escape public schools.

The Institute's research on vouchers is not a search for truth but a search for justifications for its political program. An objective research program would seek to find out if vouchers are an effective means of improving school conditions. However, the Institute's program statements indicate a belief that vouchers are the solution:

> One of the most important areas of research for our experts will be the need for school vouchers ... [Vouchers] would both improve educational performance and give the existing public school bureaucracy an

incentive to make dramatic changes in their schools in order to keep parents satisfied.[74]

Therefore, the goal of the Institute's support of research is not to prove whether vouchers are effective but to create arguments supporting voucher plans. Objective research is replaced by political polemics. This is most evident in the Institute's efforts to affect public opinion through marketing its educational experts to the media. Using its contacts in the media, the Manhattan Institute ensures that its paid scholars will be contacted for their opinions on educational policies. This results in the frequent appearance of their experts' names in newspaper stories. The Institute proudly keeps track of its media influence and lists it on its website under the categories of "National Media Attention" and "Press Releases."

The combination of the Manhattan Institute's attempts to affect public policy and the work of politicians is even evident in higher education. In 1998, New York City Mayor Rudy Giuliani appointed a seven-member task force to prepare a plan for reforming the City University of New York. Reflecting his conservative Republican views, Giuliani selected as chair of the task force Benno Schmidt, Jr., who was head of the Edison Project—the same private school corporation that would later select Manhattan Institute's Floyd Flake to lead its charter school division. Another member of the task force was Heather MacDonald, a John M. Olin Fellow at the Manhattan Institute.[75]

Another method of the Institute is to pay newspaper reporters to attend so-called informational meetings. For instance, the Institute, along with the AEI, provided research money to Herrnstein and Murray to write *The Bell Curve*, a book that purports to show the intellectual inferiority of lower social classes and African Americans. After the completion of the book, the Institute provided honoraria of $500–$1,500 to influential politicians and journalists to attend a seminar on Murray's research.[76]

The Manhattan Institute's association with *The Bell Curve* highlights some of the inherent racism in conservative arguments. A group of studies used in *The Bell Curve* was supported by the Pioneer Fund, which has been criticized for the politics of its 1937 founder, Wyckliffe Draper. Draper, a textile tycoon, was an admirer of the eugenics policies of Nazi Germany. After World War II, the Pioneer Fund provided major financial support to psychologist Arthur Jensen and physicist William Shockley, who argued that innate genetic inferiority was the cause of Black poverty and failure in school.[77]

Murray's defense for using research supported by the Pioneer Fund is stated thus:

> Never mind that the relationship between the founder of the Pioneer Fund and today's Pioneer Fund is roughly analogous to that between Henry Ford and today's Ford Foundation. The charges have been made, they have

wide currency, and some people will always believe that *The Bell Curve* rests on data concocted by neo-Nazi eugenicists.[78]

My interest is not in the statistical data used by Herrnstein and Murray to argue—I am a softheaded type who believes statistics can be manipulated to support any belief—that Whites and African Americans differ by an average of 15 IQ points. I am interested in their program recommendations, which are similar to those of other Manhattan Institute policies. For instance, Herrnstein and Murray argued that "These [differences in average IQ scores] are useful in the quest to understand why ... occupational and wage differences separate blacks and whites, or why aggressive affirmative action has produced academic apartheid in our universities."[79]

Herrnstein and Murray argued that affirmative action results in bringing many African American students onto college campuses who are unable to academically compete with White students. As a result, many African American students separate themselves from the rest of the student body and support Black Studies departments. This is what Herrnstein and Murray mean by "academic apartheid." Their answer to current affirmative-action policies is to treat people as individuals and to apply the same standards to all students. They also believe that the current form of affirmative action results in the dumbing down of curricula and textbooks and the spread of multiculturalism.

Herrnstein and Murray contended that financial and social elites deserve their social positions because of their superior average IQs. With regard to educational policies, their concern is not with the average student, who they feel receives an adequate education commensurate with his or her IQ, but with the gifted student. In language that suggests intellectual elitism and educational concerns, they contended:

> It needs to be said openly: The people who run the United States—create its jobs, expand its technologies, cure its sick, teach in its universities, administer its cultural and political and legal institutions—are drawn mainly from a thin layer of cognitive ability at the top ... It matters enormously not just that the people in the top few centiles of ability get to college ... or even that many of them go to elite colleges but that they are educated well.[80]

Using this reasoning, Herrnstein and Murray argued for the concentration of educational programs on the needs of the gifted. Furthermore, in one of the most unusual arguments for school choice, they proposed that the federal government support school choice because parents of gifted children will be the type that will select a tougher academic program. In fact, they argued that because IQ is inherited, educational ambition is primarily "concentrated among the parents of the brightest of the brightest. Policy [referring to school choice] should make it as easy as possible for them to match up with classes that satisfy their ambitions."[81]

In 2008, Charles Murray continued to stress the importance of the inheritance of intelligence in his book *Real Education*.[82] In the book, Murray argues that college is only suitable for 20 percent of the population with a more realistic number being 10 percent. In 2009, he was asked to present his ideas as part of the panel for the Manhattan Institute's Center for the American University Forum. The Manhattan Institute listed Murray's qualifications as being "W. H. Brady Scholar, American Enterprise Institute."[83] Charles Murray is listed as a Brady scholar by the AEI. The AEI established the W. H. Brady Program in 2003 and announced at the time:

> AEI [American Enterprise Institute] has established a major new program of research, conferences, student fellowships, and publications concerned with issues of freedom and culture in contemporary society. The W. H. Brady Program in Culture and Freedom has been endowed with a $15 million gift from the W. H. Brady Foundation and from Mr. Brady's daughter, Elizabeth Brady Lurie, The Brady Program will support the work of several AEI scholars, including Charles Murray, who has been appointed to the W. H. Brady Chair, and also Lynne V. Cheney [Vice President Cheney's wife].[84]

After the 2008 national elections, the Manhattan Institute continued to campaign for the Republican education agenda. In 2009, the Institute announced that its "work on education reform focuses on improving two main reforms of public education: school choice and accountability."[85] The announcement went on to describe what the Institute considered to be the two main reform movements:

> School choice reforms (including charter schools and school vouchers) are dedicated to improving the options available to parents of children in public schools, and making public schools more directly accountable to parents for education outcomes. Accountability reforms are devoted to improving educational achievement by focusing on imparting knowledge and skills and making teachers, administrators, and students accountable for success or failure.[86]

Christian Coalition: Religious Politics

In 2013, the Christian Coalition described itself as: "one of the largest conservative grassroots political organizations in America. Christian Coalition offers people of faith the vehicle to be actively involved in impacting the issues they care about – from the county courthouse to the halls of Congress."[87] The stated mission of the organization is to:

- **Represent** the pro-family point of view before local councils, school boards, state legislatures and Congress
- **Speak out** in the public arena and in the media
- **Train** leaders for effective social and political action

- **Inform** pro-family voters about timely issues and legislation.
- **Protest** anti-Christian bigotry and defend the rights of people of faith.[88]

The Christian Coalition plays an important role in winning elections for candidates supporting pro-life, abstinence education, school prayer, choice plans that include religious schools, and opposition to gay/lesbian marriage.

The Christian Coalition was organized in 1989 by televangelist Pat Robertson and Ralph Reed after Pat Robertson's unsuccessful presidential campaign in 1988. Its headquarters is in Washington, DC where it can maintain close tabs on federal legislation. It immediately alerts its membership about any bill in Congress that is important to the interests of its members. Members are given the postal and e-mail addresses and the fax and telephones numbers of their Congressional representatives so that they can express their viewpoints on pending legislation. However, the real political activity is in local churches. This raises the issue of religious involvement in politics.

In 2004, the Christian Coalition provided the following justification for blending religion and politics:

> We are driven by the belief that people of faith have a right and a responsibility to be involved in the world around them. That involvement includes community, social and political action. Whether on a stump, in print, over the airways the Christian Coalition is dedicated to equipping and educating God's people with the resources and information to battle against anti-family legislation.[89]

In 2009, the Christian Coalition described its political methods, including the distribution of voter guides through churches. "Our hallmark work lies in voter education," states the Christian Coalition website.

> Each election year, Christian Coalition distributes tens of millions of voter guides throughout all fifty states, (up to seventy million in 2000 alone!). These guides help give voters a clear understanding of where candidates stand on important pro-family issues – *before they go to the polls on Election Day* [author's emphasis].[90]

Voter guides distributed through churches threaten their tax-exempt status. Therefore, the Christian Coalition provides a carefully crafted list of dos and don'ts. In the official words of the organization, "And although a church's tax status does limit the amount of political activity it may engage in, it does not prohibit a church from encouraging citizenship."[91] The Christian Coalition informs ministers that the provided list of:

> do's and don'ts will help guide you, without jeopardizing your church's tax-exempt status, as you lead your congregation into the God-given duties

of citizenship. Remember, as Edmund Burke warned, 'All that is necessary for the triumph of evil is for good men to do nothing'.[92]

The Christian Coalitions' list of permissible political actions by churches provides an actual guide to the methods ministers can use to influence their congregations:

> What Churches May Do
> Conduct non-partisan voter registration drives
> Distribute non-partisan voter education materials, such as Christian Coalition voter guides and scorecards
> Host candidate or issue forums where all viable candidates are invited and allowed to speak
> Allow candidates and elected officials to speak at church services; if one is allowed to speak, others should not be prohibited from speaking
> Educate members about pending legislation
> Lobby for legislation and may spend no more than an insubstantial amount of its budget (five percent is safe) on direct lobbying activities
> Endorse candidates in their capacity as private citizens – A pastor does not lose his right to free speech because he is an employee of a church
> Participate fully in political committees that are independent of the church.

The Christian Coalition also provides boundaries for the political action of churches:

> What Churches May Not Do
> Endorse candidates directly or indirectly from the pulpit on behalf of the church
> Contribute funds or services (such as mailing lists or office equipment) directly to candidates or political committees
> Distribute materials that clearly favor any one candidate or political party
> Pay fees for partisan political events from church funds
> Allow candidates to solicit funds while speaking in church
> Set up a political committee that would contribute funds to political candidates.[93]

The Christian Coalition joined hands with major conservative think tanks to support the Republican education agenda. Many of its education goals appear in No Child Left Behind. No Child Left Behind contains many items dear to the heart of Christian conservatives, including support of abstinence education, protection of school prayer, public funding of faith-based organizations, the Boy Scouts of America Equal Access Act, and control of internet and other forms of pornography. The Christian Coalition, along with conservative think tanks, played an important role in selling No Child Left Behind to politicians and the public.

Thomas B. Fordham Institute and the Educational Excellence Network

Chester Finn, Jr. and Diane Ravitch founded the Educational Excellence Network in 1982 which operated out of the Hudson Institute and is now a project of the Thomas B. Fordham Institute which is supported by the Thomas B. Fordham Foundation. The initial funding for the Educational Excellence Network came from the John M. Olin Foundation and the Andrew Mellon Foundation.[94] The Thomas B. Fordham Foundation was founded in 1996. In 2004, Chester Finn, Jr. was a John M. Olin Fellow at the Manhattan Institute and President of the Thomas B. Fordham Foundation. During the Ronald Reagan's presidency, Finn served between 1985 and 1988 as Assistant Secretary for Research and Improvement at the U.S. Department of Education. He was also a founding partner and senior scholar with the Edison Project.

In 2013, the Thomas B. Fordham Institute described its mission as:

> The Thomas B. Fordham Institute is the nation's leader in advancing educational excellence for every child through quality research, analysis, and commentary, as well as on-the-ground action and advocacy in Ohio.
>
> **We advance:**
>
> - High standards for schools, students and educators;
> - Quality education options for families;
> - A more productive, equitable and efficient education system; and
> - A culture of innovation, entrepreneurship, and excellence.
>
> **We promote education reform by:**
>
> - Producing rigorous policy research and incisive analysis;
> - Building coalitions with policy makers, donors, organizations and others who share our vision; and
> - Advocating bold solutions and comprehensive responses to education challenges, even when opposed by powerful interests and timid establishments.[95]

The methods used by Republicans to recruit like-minded scholars are given in a 1996 letter Finn wrote to members of the Educational Excellence Network when its work was transferred from the Hudson Institute to the Thomas B. Fordham Institute. Finn wrote:

> Fifteen years ago this autumn, Diane Ravitch and I found ourselves on the faculties of education of two major universities: Diane at Columbia's Teachers College, I at Vanderbilt's George Peabody College. And we found these lonely places indeed for people who believed in things like standards, content, basics, accountability and choices.

Surely, we said, there must be at least a few other scholars and analysts who see the education world as we do and might benefit from some sort of loose-knit "network" that would foster communications, exchange information, ideas and research findings, and also offer a touch of what psychologists might term a "support group."

So Diane hosted a meeting at Teachers College and the dozen or so people who assembled there judged that this was indeed worth trying to put together. A couple of private foundations—notably John M. Olin and Andrew Mellon—wrote modest checks to help launch our somewhat vaguely-defined venture, and off we went.[96]

The Thomas B. Fordham Institute was founded in 1959 and in 1995 its board of trustees decided to focus on school issues. In 1996 Finn became head of the Thomas B. Fordham Institute which, in turn, sponsored the Educational Excellence Network. The organization describes the relationship between the Fordham Foundation and the Institute:

In 2007, the Foundation became a "supporting organization" (in IRS terminology) of the Institute. As a result, the Institute is the public face of nearly all that Fordham does, while the Foundation uses its modest endowment primarily to support the Institute's work, supplemented by generous support from other funders.[97]

In 2009, the Institute described its work:

We promote policies that strengthen accountability and expand education options for parents and families. Our reports examine issues such as the No Child Left Behind Act, school choice and teacher quality. Our sister nonprofit, the Thomas B. Fordham Foundation, sponsors charter schools in Ohio.[98]

The Thomas B. Fordham Institute is very clear about the methods it uses to influence education policies. It focuses on the creation and dissemination of research and policies designed to influence the direction of U.S. education policies. The Institute's 2009 mission statement declares that the organization advances "reform of American education" by "engaging in solid research and provocative analysis, disseminating information and ideas that shape the debate," and "informing policy makers at every level about promising solutions to pressing education problems."[99]

From its beginnings, the Educational Excellence Network used these methods to influence government policies. It flooded the market with educational policy statements, offered briefings to public leaders, evaluated legislation and gave advice to policymakers, educators, business groups, and community leaders. The

"Hot Topics" section of the Educational Excellence Network was dominated by the writings of Finn and Ravitch. In August 1996, two articles were offered by Finn: "Charters, Charters, and Charters" and "Making Standards Matter 1996." In June 1996, there were four articles by Finn, seven articles by Ravitch, and one by Mike Garber; and in July 1996, three articles were offered by Ravitch and one by Finn.[100]

Finn's 1996 article on charter schools provides a good example of how the media are used as part of the trickle-down theory of influencing public opinion. In early August 1996, I downloaded from the Hudson Institute's website an article by Finn on charter schools.[101] Shortly after, I turned to the op-ed page of *The New York Times* and found a bold title across the top: "Beating Up on Charter Schools," by Finn, who was identified as a Fellow of the Hudson Institute and former Assistant Secretary of Education during the Reagan administration. In the article, Finn attacked the two teachers' unions for hindering the growth of charter schools.[102]

Finn also provides a good example of foundation-based scholars who are used by conservatives to implement their trickle-down theory of ideas. After earning his doctorate in education policy and administration at Harvard University, Finn became a Professor of Education at Vanderbilt University in 1981 and, while on leave from Vanderbilt, he served in a variety of government positions before becoming Assistant Secretary for Research and Improvement as well as counselor to Secretary of Education William Bennett from 1985 to 1988. After Bush replaced Reagan as President, Finn returned to Vanderbilt. In 1994, while still on leave from Vanderbilt, Finn was appointed John M. Olin Fellow at the Hudson Institute and then in 1996 became President of the Thomas B. Fordham Institute.[103]

Ravitch is another foundation and government-based scholar. Ravitch served as Assistant Secretary of Education as well as counselor to the Secretary of Education from 1991 to 1993 and later became a senior research scholar at New York University and a senior Fellow at the Manhattan Institute. Currently she is a research Professor of Education at New York University and senior fellow at the Hoover Institution at Stanford University and the Brookings Institution.[104]

With the support of these think tanks, Finn and Ravitch flooded the market with articles and books containing the Republican education message. Besides more than 200 articles in professional and popular journals, Finn has written ten books, including *Radical Education Reform*; *We Must Take Charge: Our Schools and Our Future*; and *Scholars, Dollars and Bureaucrats*. With Ravitch, Finn coauthored *What Do Our 17-Year-Olds Know?*[105] Ravitch has also written more than 200 articles for the popular and scholarly press, and six books, including *National Standards in American Education: A Citizen's Guide 1995*; *The Schools We Deserve*; and *The Great School Wars: New York City, 1805–1973*.[106] More recently, Ravitch reversed her earlier support for national standards and testing in *The Death and Life of the Great American School System: How Testing and Choice Are Undermining Education.*[107]

The Republican philosophy of Finn, with its combination of free-market thinking and the use of government authority to impose social order, was captured in a statement by Finn in a book review. The reviewed book advocated the complete separation of school and state. In reference to complete abolition of the government's role in education, Finn stated, "I don't share the author's hostility to standards, curricula and assessments set by policymakers, but I resonate with his ideas about freeing schools from state control of management and freeing families to select the education that suits them."[108]

In a similar fashion, Ravitch argued that the academic standards of public schools declined in the 1960s and 1970s as a result of demands by civil rights groups for equality of educational opportunity and because of capitulation by educational administrators to student rebels. Reacting to the permissiveness of the 1960s and 1970s, Ravitch believed the key to school improvement is the re-establishment of educational authority through imposition of government academic standards and achievement tests.[109]

Republicans, Business, and Human Capital

Similar to Democrats, Republicans were enamored with human capital theories. Particularly the Party's business supporters turned to human capital theory to justify educational policies that would improve the quality of their workers. A traditional Republican concern is the impact of schooling on the economic system. During the 1950s, the National Manpower Council played a major role in defining the human capital policies of the Republican Party. Founded in 1951, the National Manpower Council, reflecting the technological needs of the Cold War, recommended in its first report in 1951 that Selective Service deferments should be used "to insure a continuous supply of college-trained people whose general education and specialized knowledge are essential to the nation's civilian and military strength."[110] In 1953, the council issued *A Policy for Scientific and Professional Manpower* which warned that the Soviet Union's totalitarian methods were forcing large numbers of students to study science and engineering, which would make the Soviet Union superior in technology and military weaponry. The problem facing the U.S. was persuading more talented youth to enter technological fields.[111]

The Soviet launching of Sputnik in 1957 seemed to confirm the warnings of the National Manpower Council. Within a month of the Sputnik launch, Republican President Eisenhower called on the U.S. school system to educate more scientists and engineers to match the large numbers being graduated by the Soviet educational system. "My scientific advisers," Eisenhower declared, "place [the shortage of scientists and engineers] above all other immediate tasks of producing missiles, of developing new techniques in the armed services."[112] Convinced that the education of more scientists and engineers was the key to winning the Cold War, Eisenhower proposed the National Defense Education Act, which was passed by Congress in 1958.

It is ironic that despite Republicans' rhetoric against big government and federal involvement in local schools, they sponsored legislation which included federal support of scholarships, student loans, support for the development of new math and science curricula for public schools, and aid for recruiting more teachers. Republican concerns with human capital development continued into the 1970s, when Republican President Richard Nixon supported federal grants for career education programs. Nixon hoped that career education would create a closer alignment of the public school curriculum with the needs of the labor market. Within this framework, public schools would convince students to think about education in relation to a future job; to focus their learning on the skills required for that job; and then, after graduation, to move smoothly into the labor market.[113]

In 1983, in a report titled *Action for Excellence*, business leaders joined the chorus for school reform to meet the needs of global competition. The report was issued by the Education Commission of the States' Task Force on Education for Economic Growth, which was composed of representatives of major corporations and governors. Its funding came from some of the largest corporations, including IBM and Xerox, whose chief executives were Louis V. Gerstner, Jr. and David Kearns. Supporting an increased role for business in educational change, *Action for Excellence* asserts: "If the business community gets more involved in both the design and delivery of education, we are going to become more competitive as an economy."[114]

In 1994, Gerstner, CEO and chairman of IBM, explained that he "wanted to go beyond traditional business partnerships that enhance schools by providing equipment, mentors, or increased opportunities . . . While these generous efforts may brighten the picture for a few children, they do not change 'the system'."[115] Claiming that his interest in educational reform "is fueled by intense anger, and frustration," Gerstner emphatically asserted that: "You know that most young applicants are not qualified to do today's more intellectually demanding jobs, let alone tomorrow's."[116]

Republicans were not alone in supporting business involvement in public schools. In 1996, President Bill Clinton welcomed 49 corporate chiefs and 40 governors to a national education summit held at IBM's conference center in Palisades, New York. Hosting the event were Gerstner and Wisconsin's Republican Governor Tommy Thompson. Both Republicans and New Democrats welcomed the summit meeting's emphasis on creating national and state academic standards.[117]

Conclusion

Both the 2013 National Republican Committee and the 2012 Republican platform criticize federal involvement in state and local schools and promote choice with vouchers, debit cards, or tax credits. In this situation, the Republicans act as a countervailing force to the Democrat's support of the Common Core State Standards and the creation of a national student database in the form of inBloom.

In the past, conservative Republicans have effectively marketed their ideas through think tanks, foundations, and policy-interested nongovernment groups. Conservative think tanks marketed their ideas about school choice by financing conservative-oriented research and by using public relations methods to influence media, politicians, and the general public. However, the work of Republican think tanks also highlights an important difference between Republicans and religious conservatives. Religious conservatives are often hesitant about the government imposing national academic standards and testing because of concerns about schools teaching secular humanism. They want to rely on the authority of God. School choice would provide religious conservatives with this opportunity. In contrast, Republicans, such as Doyle, Finn, and Ravitch, believe that school choice will create more efficient ways of implementing government-established national academic goals and standards.

It is important to emphasize that a conscious effort is being made to disseminate ideas and influence public opinion by conservative think tanks, such as the Manhattan Institute, The Heritage Foundation, the Thomas B. Fordham Foundation and the AEI. Their influence is the result of calculated planning by conservative intellectuals and businesspeople.

In 1986, at a celebration of the accomplishments of The Heritage Foundation, Republican President Ronald Reagan recognized the importance of conservative influences on public opinion. After paying homage to Austrian economists Friedrich Hayek and Ludwig von Mises, Reagan recalled the argument made by Richard Weaver in the 1948 book *Ideas Have Consequences*. Reagan told those celebrating the work of The Heritage Foundation: "It goes back to what Richard Weaver had said and what Heritage is all about. Ideas do have consequences, rhetoric is policy, and words are action."[118]

Notes

1 Republican National Committee, "RESOLUTION CONCERNING COMMON CORE EDUCATION STANDARDS." Retrieved from https://docs.google.com/file/d/0B558bfJRCLuuOXdsVXJmZy1IRms/edit?pli=1 on April 18, 2013.
2 Michael J. Petrilli, "The RNC on the CCSSI, OMG!" (April 18, 2013). Retrieved from http://www.edexcellence.net/commentary/education-gadfly-daily/flypaper/2013/the-rnc-on-the-ccssi-omg.html on April 19, 2012.
3 Republican National Committee, "RESOLUTION CONCERNING COMMON CORE STANDARDS."

4 2012 Republican Platform, "We Believe in America," p. 12. Retrieved from http://www.gop.com/2012-republican-platform_home/ on April 19, 2013.

5 Ibid., p. 35.

6 Republican National Committee, "RESOLUTION CONCERNING COMMON CORE STANDARDS."

7 Ibid.

8 Ibid.

9 Ibid.

10 Ibid.

11 2012 Republican Platform, "We Believe in America," p. 35.

12 Ibid.

13 Lauren McGaughy, "Voucher Program Heads to State Supreme Court on Tuesday; No Immediate Ruling Expected," *The Times-Picayune* (March 18, 2013). Retrieved from http://blog.nola.com/politics/print.html?entry=/2013/03/jindal_voucher_louisiana_orlea.html on April 1, 2013.

14 Stephanie Simon, "Indiana Court Upholds Broadest School Voucher Program," Reuters (March 26, 2013). Retrieved from http://www.reuters.com/article/2013/03/26/us-usa-education-vouchers-idUSBRE92P0TN20130326 on April 2, 2013.

15 Anne Ryman, "Expansion of State's School-Voucher System Takes Effect Today," *The Republic* (January 1, 2013). Retrieved from http://www.azcentral.com/news/articles/20130101arizona-school-voucher-system.html on April 2, 2013.

16 Murray N. Rothbard, *Man, Economy, and State: A Treatise of Economic Principles* (Los Angeles: Nash, 1970).

17 See Peter Boettke, "Friedrich A. Hayek (1899–1992)." Retrieved from the Department of Economics, New York University, http//www.peter-boettke.com/research/edited-books/the-legacy-of-f-a-hayek-politics-philosophy-and-economics/ on August 2, 2000.

18 Friedrich Hayek, *The Road to Serfdom* (Chicago: University of Chicago Press, 1994).

19 Milton Friedman, *Capital and Freedom* (Chicago: University of Chicago Press, 1962), p. 89.

20 Ibid., p. 92.

21 Public Law 107–110, 107th Congress, January 8, 2002 [H.R. 1], "No Child Left Behind Act of 2001," p. 58.

22 Ibid., p. 122.

23 Ibid., pp. 58, 70, 122, 185, 201, 206, 219, 232, 248, 297, 382, 419, 584, 657.

24 Arthur M. Schlesinger, Jr., *The Disuniting of America* (Knoxville, TN: Whittle Direct Books, 1991), p. 8.

25 James Traub, "Has Benno Schmidt Learned His Lesson?", *New York Times*, 31 October 1994, pp. 51–59.

26 Ibid.

27 Ibid., p. 58.

28 EdisonLearning "Corporate History." Retrieved from http://www.edisonlearning.com/about_us/corporate_history.be on April 12, 2009.

29 EdisonLearning, "About." Retrieved from http://edisonlearning.com/about-edisonlearning on April 23, 2013.

30 James Smith, *The Idea Brokers and the Rise of the New Policy Elite* (New York: Free Press, 1991), p. 181.

31 William Simon, *A Time for Truth* (New York: Readers Digest Press, 1978), p. 233.

32 Ibid., p. xii.

33 Ibid., p. xii.

34 Ibid., pp. 232–233.

35 Ibid., p. 230; Smith, *The Idea Brokers and the Rise of the New Policy Elite*, p. 182.

36 Smith, *The Idea Brokers and the Rise of the New Policy Elite*, p. 182.

37 David M. Ricci, *The Transformation of American Politics: The New Washington and the Rise of Think Tanks* (New Haven, CT: Yale University Press, 1993), p. 166.
38 The Heritage Foundation, "About." Retrieved from http://www.askheritage.org/about on April 23, 2013.
39 The Heritage Foundation, "Become a Member Today." Retrieved from http://www.askheritage.org/about on April 23, 2013.
40 Smith, *The Idea Brokers and the Rise of the New Policy Elite*, p. 197.
41 Ibid., pp. 197–202.
42 Chester E. Finn and Diane Ravitch, "Magna Charter? A Report Card on School Reform in 1995," *Policy Review* (Fall 1995), p. 74; Dinesh D'Souza, "We the Slaveowners: In Jefferson's America, Were Some Men Not Created Equal?", *Policy Review* (Fall 1995), p. 74.
43 D'Souza, "We the Slaveowners: In Jefferson's America, Were Some Men Not Created Equal?", p. 74.
44 Lindsey M. Burke and Rachel Sheffield, "Universal Preschool's Empty Promises," The Heritage Foundation (March 12, 2013). Retrieved from http://www.heritage.org/research/reports/2013/03/universal-preschools-empty-promises on April 23, 2013.
45 Lindsey M. Burke, ed., "Choosing to Succeed," The Heritage Foundation (2013). Retrieved from http://www.heritage.org/research/reports/2013/01/choosing-to-succeed-choosing-to-succeed on April 23, 2013.
46 Ibid.
47 Ibid.
48 Matthew Spalding, "Character and the Destiny of Free Government," *Building A Culture of Character, Heritage Lectures* (Washington, DC: The Heritage Foundation, 2002).
49 Ibid.
50 Quoted in Smith, *The Idea Brokers and the Rise of the New Policy Elite*, p. 178.
51 American Enterprise Institute, "Policy Studies." Retrieved from http://www.aei.org/policy/ on April 23, 2013.
52 Michael Q. McShane, "What Research Tells Us About School Vouchers" (February 27, 2013), The Heritage Foundation. Retrieved from http://www.aei.org/speech/education/k-12/what-research-tells-us-about-school-vouchers/ on April 23, 2013.
53 Grace Smith, "What Parents Should Know for Back to School," WebMemo #561 (September 3, 2004), p. 1. Retrieved from www.heritage.org on July 24, 2005.
54 "No Child Left Behind: Mend It, End It, or Let It Work?" Retrieved from http://www.aei.org/speech/education/no-child-left-behind-speech/ on July 24, 2005.
55 Ibid.
56 Ibid.
57 Dan Lips, "Reforming No Child Left Behind by Allowing States to Opt Out: An A-Plus for Federalism," *Backgrounder* (Washington, DC: The Heritage Foundation, June 19, 2007), p. 1.
58 Dan Lips, Jennifer Marshall, and Lindsey Burke, *A Parent's Guide to Education Reform* (Washington, DC: The Heritage Foundation, 2007).
59 Ibid., pp. 13–29.
60 "Race to the Top? The Promise—and—Challenges of Charter School Growth." Retrieved from http://www.ewa.org/site/News2?news_iv_ctrl=-1&cmd=articles&page=NewsArticle&id=6811&start=2 on April 8, 2009.
61 Ibid.
62 Manhattan Institute for Policy Research, "Home." Retrieved from http://www.manhattan-institute.org/ on May 6, 2013.
63 Marcus Winters, "About Urban Education Improving Urban Education: Getting Charter Schools Right," Manhattan Institute for Policy Research. Retrieved from http://www.manhattan-institute.org/html/csll_urban_education.htm on May 6, 2013.
64 Ibid.

65 Manhattan Institute for Policy Research. Retrieved from http://www.manhattan-institute.org/ on January 5, 2005.
66 Manhattan Institute for Policy Research, "About the Center for Civic Innovation at the Manhattan Institute: Educational Reform." Retrieved from http://www.manhattan-institute.org/html/miarticle.htm?id=6024 on January 5, 2005.
67 Manhattan Institute for Policy Research, "About the Manhattan Institute." Retrieved from http://www.manhattan-institute.org/html/about_mi_30.htm on January 5, 2005.
68 Ibid.
69 Manhattan Institute for Policy Research, "Sponsoring the Manhattan Institute." Retrieved from http://www.manhattan-institute.org/ on January 5, 2005.
70 Edward Wyatt, "Floyd Flake to Take Post With Education Company" (May 3, 2000). Retrieved from http://www.nytimes.com/2000/05/03/nyregion/floyd-flake-to-take-post-with-education-company.html on March 29, 2001.
71 Manhattan Institute for Policy Research, "Program Areas: Educational Reform." Retrieved from http://www.manhattan-institute.org/ on January 5, 2005.
72 Manhattan Institute for Policy Research, "An Evaluation of the Florida A-Plus Accountability and School Choice." Retrieved from http://www.manhattan-institute.org/ on January 5, 2005.
73 Manhattan Institute for Policy Research, "Program Areas: Educational Reform."
74 Ibid.
75 Karen W. Arenson, "With CUNY Study, Ex-Yale Chief Seeks New View of Public Colleges," *The New York Times* (August 30, 1998). Retrieved from http://www.nytimes.com/1998/08/30/nyregion/with-cuny-study-ex-yale-chief-seeks-new-view-of-public-colleges.html on July 9, 2013.
76 As reported in Michael Lind, *Up From Conservatism: Why the Right Is Wrong for America* (New York: Free Press, 1996), p. 182.
77 Ibid., p. 197.
78 Richard J. Herrnstein and Charles Murray, *The Bell Curve: Intelligence and Class Structure in American Life* (New York: Free Press, 1994), p. 562.
79 Ibid., p. 562.
80 Ibid., p. 418.
81 Ibid., p. 441.
82 Charles Murray, *Real Education: Four Simple Truths for Bringing America's Schools Back to Reality* (New York: Crown Forum, 2008).
83 Manhattan Institute, Center for the American University Forum: Panel II, "The University Of The Future" (February 5, 2009). Retrieved from http://www.manhattan-institute.org/html/mi_recent_events.htm on May 2, 2009.
84 American Enterprise Institute, "AEI Establishes W. H. Brady Program in Culture and Freedom" (May 21, 2003). Retrieved from http://www.aei.org/search/AEI+Establishes+W.+H.+Brady+Program+in+Culture+and+Freedom on May 2, 2009.
85 Center for Civic Innovation at the Manhattan Institute, "About the Center for Civic Innovation: Education Reform." Retrieved from http://www.manhattan-institute.org/html/cci.htm#02 on April 9, 2009.
86 Ibid.
87 Christian Coalition, "About Us." Retrieved from http://www.cc.org/about_us on May 6, 2013.
88 Ibid.
89 Christian Coalition, "About Us." Retrieved from http://www.cc.org/about_us on March 5, 2004.
90 Christian Coalition, "About Us." Retrieved from http://www.cc.org/about_us on April 10, 2009.
91 Christian Coalition, "Dos and Don'ts." Retrieved from http://www.cc.org on March 2, 2005.

92 Ibid.

93 Ibid.

94 Chester Finn, Jr. describes the development of the Educational Excellence Network in Chester Finn, Jr., "Farewell—and Hello Again (Finn's Last Stand)." Retrieved from http://www.edexcellence.net/foundation/publication/publication.cfm?id=188 on January 8, 2000.

95 Thomas B. Fordham Institute, "About Us." Retrieved from http://www.edexcellence.net/about-us/fordham-mission.html on May 6, 2013.

96 Ibid.

97 Ibid.

98 Ibid.

99 Thomas B. Fordham Institute, "Fordham Mission." Retrieved from http://www.edexcellence.net/about-us/fordham-mission.html on July 9, 2013.

100 This information was retrieved from http://www.edexcellence.net on September 24, 1998.

101 Chester Finn, Bruno V. Manno, and Gregg Vanourek, *Charter Schools in Action: Renewing Public Education* (Princeton: Princeton University Press, 2001).

102 Chester Finn, Jr., "Beating Up on Charter Schools" (August 24, 1996), *The New York Times*, p. A23.

103 Thomas B. Fordham Institute, "Fordham Staff: Chester Finn, Jr." Retrieved from http://www.edexcellence.net/about-us/fordham-staff/chester-e-finn-jr.html on April 6, 2009.

104 "Diane Ravitch: Curriculum Vitae." Retrieved from http://www.dianeravitch.com/vita.html on April 11, 2009.

105 Thomas B. Fordham Institute, "Fordham Staff: Chester Finn, Jr."

106 "Diane Ravitch: Curriculum Vitae."

107 Diane Ravitch, *The Death and Life of the Great American School System: How Testing and Choice Are Undermining Education* (New York: Basic Books, 2011).

108 Chester E. Finn, Jr., "Finn on Ravitch: A Review of The Death and Life of the Great American School System" (March 10, 2010). Retrieved from http://www.edexcellence.net/ohio-policy/gadfly/2010/march-10/finn-on-ravitch-a-review-of-the-death-and-life-of-the-great-american-school-system.html on July 9, 2013.

109 See Diane Ravitch, *The Troubled Crusade: American Education 1945–1980* (New York: Basic Books, 1983).

110 National Manpower Council, *Student Deferment and National Manpower Policy* (New York: Columbia University Press, 1951), pp. 8–9.

111 National Manpower Council, *A Policy for Scientific and Professional Manpower* (New York: Columbia University Press, 1953).

112 Dwight D. Eisenhower, "Our Future Security," in *Science and Education for National Defense: Hearings Before the Committee on Labor and Public Welfare, United States Senate, Eighty-Fifth Congress, Second Session* (Washington, DC: U.S. Government Printing Office, 1958), p. 1360.

113 See Joel Spring, *The Sorting Machine Revisited: National Educational Policy Since 1945*, Second Edition (White Plains, NY: Longman, 1989), pp. 151–155.

114 Task Force on Education for Economic Growth, *Action for Excellence* (Denver, CO: Education Commission of the States, 1983), p. 18.

115 Louis Gerstner, Jr., with Roger D. Semerad, Denis Philip Doyle, and William Johnston, *Reinventing Education: Entrepreneurship in America's Public Schools* (New York: Dutton, 1994), p. ix.

116 Ibid., pp. ix–x.

117 Millicent Lawton, "Summit Accord Calls for Focus on Standards," *Education Week*, April 3, 1996, pp. 1, 14–15.

118 Quoted in Smith, *The Idea Brokers and the Rise of the New Policy Elite*, p. 20.

4
THE REPUBLICAN EDUCATION AGENDA

The Culture Wars

Social issues continue to be an important part of the Republican education agenda. These social issues are components of the Republican master narrative as detailed by Drew Westin in *The Political Brain*. Westin identifies these components of the Republican master narrative that are related to the Republican education agenda:

- Republicans protect traditional American values
- Republicans protect traditional religious faith and values
- Poverty is the result of poor character and every American has the chance to be financially successful through hard work
- Republicans protect the free market and rely on the "invisible hand" of the market
- Republicans protect individual freedom from regulation by big government.[1]

Social Issues 2012 Campaign

As I will detail later in this chapter, Republicans have supported English First in opposition to bilingual instruction designed to maintain other languages along with teaching English. The 2012 Republican platform states: "To ensure that all students have access to the mainstream of American life, we support the English First approach and oppose divisive programs that limit students' ability to advance in American society."[2] Traditionally, Republicans have opposed school programs designed to maintain other languages and cultures which some Republicans claim breeds ethnic and racial tensions.

Also, Republicans have supported abstinence-only sex education in opposition to instruction about birth control. As stated in the 2012 Republican platform:

> We renew our call for replacing "family planning" programs for teens with abstinence education which teaches abstinence until marriage as the responsible and respected standard of behavior. Abstinence from sexual activity is the only protection that is 100 percent effective against out-of-wedlock pregnancies and sexually-transmitted diseases including HIV/AIDS when transmitted sexually. It is effective, science-based, and empowers teens to achieve optimal health outcomes and avoid risks of sexual activity. We oppose school-based clinics that provide referrals, counseling, and related services for abortion and contraception.[3]

Traditionally, Republicans have supported an emphasis on teaching American values as was again expressed in the 2012 Republican platform, which called for a "renewed focus on the Constitution and the writings of the Founding Fathers, and an accurate account of American history that celebrates the birth of this great nation."[4]

In Chapter 3, I discussed a conservative belief in the existence of a "liberal establishment" controlling the dissemination of knowledge in the U.S. This belief justified the creation of conservative think tanks and foundations to act as a countervailing force against this liberal influence. In the 2012 Republican platform, universities and colleges are targeted as bastions of "the Left" monopolizing the dissemination of ideas. The platform claims there is an ideological bias in universities that should be corrected by public university authorities:

> Ideological bias is deeply entrenched within the current university system. Whatever the solution in private institutions may be, in State institutions the trustees have a responsibility to the public to ensure that their enormous investment is not abused for political indoctrination. We call on State officials to ensure that our public colleges and universities be places of learning and the exchange of ideas, not zones of intellectual intolerance favoring the Left.[5]

The Republican Education Agenda and the Culture Wars

It was during the Reagan years that Republicans began to speak out against multiculturalism and forms of bilingual education designed to maintain minority languages and cultures. It was Republican President Reagan's Secretary of Education William Bennett who voiced the strongest objections to multiculturalism which he felt was undermining American values. In 1986, Bennett made a name for himself in academic circles when he launched a public attack against the Stanford University faculty for replacing a freshman undergraduate course entitled "Western Culture," in which students read 15 works in Western philosophy and literature, with a course entitled "Cultures, Ideas, and Values," in which readings included works by "women, minorities, and persons of color."[6] Bennett argued that students should be required to study Western culture because it provided the framework for American government and culture. In addition, he stated, "Probably most difficult for the critics of Western culture to acknowledge is that 'the West is good'." Western culture, according to Bennett, has "set the moral, political, economic, and social standards for the rest of the world."[7]

Bennett blamed the "liberal elite," a code phrase for culturally influential Democrats, for the advancement of multiculturalism, and the undermining of traditional American values. Bennett argued that the culture wars were between the beliefs held by most citizens and "the beliefs of a liberal elite that today dominates many of our institutions and who therefore exert influence on American life and culture."[8] This liberal elite, according to Bennett, inhabited universities, the literary and artistic worlds, liberal religious institutions, and the media. The liberal elite, Bennett contended, was different from former bourgeois elites, who valued the importance of the family, public morality, hard work, and individual entrepreneurship. In contrast, the liberal elite rejected many traditional Christian values and looked with scorn on Americans who believe in the value of hard work and economic individualism. Furthermore, this liberal elite supported ideas that were an anathema to the religiously oriented Republicans, such as multiculturalism, sexual freedom, and gay and lesbian relationships.

Another Reagan appointee Lynne Cheney, the wife of the future Republican Vice-President Dick Cheney, carried the banner of protecting traditional American values against the threat of multiculturalism. She shared with William Bennett a similar philosophy about the humanities. President Reagan made Cheney the head of the National Endowment for the Humanities where she served from 1986 to 1993. This gave her an important role in influencing research and writing about American culture and specifically about American history. In September, 1987, Cheney issued "American Memory: A Report on the Humanities in the Nation's Public Schools."[9] In the report she criticized history instruction in public schools:

> Long relied upon to transmit knowledge of the past to upcoming generations, our schools today appear to be about a different task. Instead of preserving the past, they more often disregard it, sometimes in the name of "progress"——the idea that today has little to learn from yesterday.[10]

She criticized the emphasis on social studies in contrast to teaching individual disciplines, such as history, political science, economics, and geography. "The culprit is 'progress'," Cheney wrote, "the belief that we can teach them how to understand the world in which they live without conveying to them the events and ideas that have brought it into existence." In her conclusion, she warned, "we run the danger of unwittingly proscribing our own heritage."[11]

The 1996 Republican platform offered a specific remedy for those fearing a loss of traditional American culture: "To reinforce our American heritage, we believe our nation's Governors, State legislators, and local school boards should support requiring our public schools to dedicate one full day each year solely to studying the Declaration of Independence and the Constitution."[12] The 1996 Republican platform, which directly attacked Democratic President Bill Clinton for not limiting bilingual education to being solely a method for learning English, stated:

> We condemn Bill Clinton's refusal, once again, to protect and preserve the most precious symbol of our Republic. English, our common language, provides a shared foundation which has allowed people from every corner of the world to come together to build the American nation.[13]

During the 1996 campaign, Republican candidate Bob Dole said:

> For more than two centuries now, English has been a force for unity, indispensable to the process of transforming untold millions of immigrants from all parts of the globe into citizens of the most open and free society the world has ever seen.[14]

Specifically emphasizing bilingual education as a method to be used only for learning English, the 1996 Republican platform related the bilingual issue to making English the official U.S. language: "For newcomers, learning the English language has always been the fastest route to the mainstream of American life. That should be the goal of bilingual education programs. We support the official recognition of English as the nation's common language."[15]

In the 2000 presidential campaign, future Republican President George W. Bush advocated cultural unity and opposed bilingual education. Bilingual education had become a symbol for a multicultural society. Also, there was concern about patriotism and flag worship, particularly with reported incidents of flag burning. The 2000 Republican platform called for cultural unity and protection of the national flag:

> Our country's ethnic diversity within a shared national culture is unique in all the world. We benefit from our differences, but we must also strengthen the ties that bind us to one another. Foremost among those is the flag. Its deliberate desecration is not "free speech" but an assault against both our proud history and our greatest hopes.[16]

The 2008 Republican platform, as per the 2012 platform, continued stressing English as a culturally unifying language. The 2008 platform stated:

> Another sign of our unity is the role of English as our common language. It has enabled people from every corner of the world to come together to build this nation. For newcomers, it has always been the fastest route to the mainstream of American life. English empowers.[17]

And the platform emphasized, "That is why fluency in *English must be the goal of bilingual education programs*. We support the recognition of English as the nation's common language [author's emphasis]."[18]

Standards and Tests: The Politics of Culture

Protecting traditional American values became an issue with the creation of academic standards for history and the content for standardized history tests. In the development of national standards and tests in the 1990s, history proved to be the most politically contentious subject. Because history is shaped by and contains political values, the debate over history standards reflects broad divisions in political ideas. In 1986, foreshadowing the national standards debate over history, California Superintendent of Public Instruction, Bill Honig, appointed Diane Ravitch, who at the time was an adjunct Professor at Teachers College, Columbia University, and Charlotte Crabtree, a Professor of Education at UCLA, to a panel to rewrite the state social studies curriculum. Ravitch would later be appointed in 1991 by President George H. W. Bush as Assistant Secretary of Education and Counselor to Secretary of Education Lamar Alexander. After her appointment to the U.S. Department of Education, Ravitch promoted "the creation of academic standards."[19]

In 1987, California officials approved a framework for the teaching of history that was primarily written by Ravitch and Crabtree.[20] The controversy was about the California framework which centered on its portrayal of the U.S. as a land of immigrants. The debate also occurred in New York with Arthur Schlesinger, Jr. and Diane Ravitch playing a major role.[21] The dispute highlights significant differences regarding the teaching and interpretation of U.S. history. For socially conservative Republicans, the major purpose in public school history instruction was creating national unity by teaching a common set of political and social values. These common values, according to this conservative approach, should be a reflection of the beliefs underlying American institutions. In Arthur Schlesinger's words:

> For better or worse, the White Anglo-Saxon Protestant tradition was for two centuries, and in crucial respects still is, the dominant influence on American culture and society . . . The language of the new nation, its laws,

its institutions, its political ideas, its literature, its customs, its precepts, its prayers, primarily derived from Britain.[22]

Using similar words, California Superintendent Bill Honig stated:

This country has been able to celebrate pluralism but keep some sense of the collective that holds us together . . . Democracy has certain core ideas, freedom of speech, law, procedural rights, the way we deal with each other.[23]

From a conservative perspective, the teaching of core values would help reduce racial and ethnic strife and ensure the perpetuation of traditional American values. Within this framework, the content of U.S. history should emphasize the common struggles and benefits received from U.S. institutions by the diverse cultural groups composing its population. The study of differing cultures in the U.S., such as Native American and African, should emphasize tolerance and unity under common institutions.

An objection to the California framework came from Nathan Huggins, a Harvard Professor of African American studies and history at Harvard. Huggins warned, "A stress on 'common culture' turns history into a tool of national unity, mandated principally by those anxious about national order and coherence."[24] There was outrage among some African Americans, Mexican Americans, and Native Americans at the concept of the U.S. being a land of immigrants. All three groups could claim to be unwilling members of U.S. society who were forced into participation by slavery and conquest. From this perspective, the history of the U.S. was marked by White violence against Africans, Mexicans, Asians, and Native Americans.

Stanford University Professor of African and Afro-American studies, Sylvia Wynter, argued that the California history framework "does not move outside the conceptual field of our present essentially Euro American cultural model."[25] The framework, she argued, did not provide a means for understanding the plight of minority groups in the U.S. Wynter asked:

How did the dispossession of the indigenous peoples, their subordination, and the mass enslavement of the people of Black African descent come to seem "just and virtuous" actions to those who affected them? How does the continuance of this initial dispossession, in the jobless, alcohol ridden reservations, the jobless drug and crime ridden inner cities . . . still come to seem to all of us, as just, or at the very least, to be in the nature of things?[26]

Joyce King, then a Santa Clara University Education Professor and one of the leading critics of the California framework, was particularly disturbed by the "we are all immigrants" interpretation of U.S. history. King called this approach "dysconscious racism . . . an impaired consciousness or a distorted way of thinking about race ... [that] tacitly accepts dominant White norms and privileges."[27] The California framework, she argued, presented a triumphant chronological history progressing to an inevitable point when all groups are able to acquire the supposed "superior" values of White Anglo-Saxon society. In this context, national unity required that all cultural groups recognize the advantages of White Anglo-Saxon traditions.

The California controversy foreshadowed later discussions about the politics of knowledge. After Diane Ravitch's appointment, in 1991, as Assistant Secretary of Education in charge of the Office of Educational Research and Improvement, Charlotte Crabtree's National Center for History in Schools received a joint award of $1.6 million to develop national history standards from Ravitch's office and the National Endowment of the Humanities headed by Lynne Cheney.

To the horror of Ravitch and Cheney, the first set of national standards in history contained teaching examples, which in the words of Cheney, "make it sound as if everything in America is wrong and grim." She complained that the teaching examples contained 17 references to the Ku Klux Klan and 19 references to McCarthyism, whereas there was no mention of Paul Revere, Thomas Edison, and other "politically incorrect White males."[28] The teaching examples were done outside the conservative political fold by Carol Gluck, a Professor of History at Columbia University. Using what she called a democratic process, Gluck spent two years meeting with more than 6,000 parents, teachers, business people, and school administrators.[29] Outraged, Lynne Cheney founded a Washington-based Committee to Review National Standards to apply political pressure for a revision of the history standards.

In 1995, the National Center for History in the Schools announced that it was revising the history standards and teaching examples. Claiming a victory, Diane Ravitch hoped that "we can declare this particular battlefront in the culture wars to be ended."[30] In reporting Ravitch's statement, Karen Diegmueller explained that Ravitch was "a panelist who not only had criticized the documents but had commissioned their creation when she served as an assistant secretary in the U.S. Department of Education."[31] Diegmueller reported that the criticisms of the history standards were primarily from conservative Republicans who contended, in Diegmueller's words, that "the standards undercut the great figures that traditionally have dominated the landscape of history and portray the United States and the West as oppressive regimes that have victimized women, minorities, and third world countries."[32] What the critics wanted, Diegmueller wrote, was a history that emphasized U.S. accomplishments and provided students with uplifting ideals.

With a cynical tone, Diegmueller opened a later *Education Week* article with these words: "Timbuktu has disappeared. Pearl Harbor has ascended. George Washington is in; Eleanor Roosevelt is out. And names and places like Joseph McCarthy and Seneca Falls, N.Y., whose prominence irked critics ... have been allotted one mention apiece."[33] Also, she reported an attempt to give a more upbeat tone to the introductions to the ten eras of U.S. history delimited by the standards.

In their 1996 campaign book, Republican candidates Bob Dole and Jack Kemp joined the chorus demanding a more upbeat history be taught in public schools. Dole and Kemp declared: "Where schools should instill an appreciation of our country and its history, often they seem to reflect a blindness toward America and its finer moments."[34]

There was even an upbeat attempt to make slavery sound positive. Sponsored by the conservative The Heritage Foundation and published in their monthly *Policy Review* was a 1995 article by Dinesh D'Souza, who at the time was the John M. Olin Scholar at another conservative think tank, the AEI. D'Souza's article was titled, "We the Slaveowners: In Jefferson's America, Were Some Men Not Created Equal?" It provides a positive slant to American slavery with the interesting conclusion, "Slavery was an institution that was terrible to endure for slaves, but it left the descendants of slaves better off in America. For this, the American Founders are owed a measure of respect and gratitude."[35]

D'Souza's major contribution to the conservative cultural argument was his 1991 book *Illiberal Education* criticizing affirmative action and multicultural education.[36] The research and writing for the book was supported by the conservative AEI and John M. Olin Foundation. Attacking the supposed domination of politically correct thinking on American college campuses, D'Souza argued that affirmative action was destructive of minority students and the quality of education. Affirmative action, he argued, results in colleges admitting many poorly prepared minority students. "The consequence," he claimed, was "minority students placed in 'high risk' intellectual environments where they compete against vastly better-prepared students, and where their probability of graduation is known to be low."[37] D'Souza argued that multiculturalism and feminism were destroying liberal education through the replacement in college courses of significant books written by White males with inferior books written by minorities and women.

The struggle over traditional American values continued into the 21st century. In 2004, the conservative Thomas B. Fordham Institute published Diane Ravitch's *A Consumer's Guide to High School History Textbooks*.[38] The book reviewed 13 American and World History textbooks for senior high schools. The reviews were written by a group of scholars who were asked if the textbooks were biased. None of the reviewers found a *conservative* bias to the books. However, some books were charged with being "left-liberal" and "leftist." For instance, Morton Keller, Spector Professor of History at Brandeis University asserted that Gary B. Nash's *American Odyssey: The United States in the Twentieth Century* is "the most biased and partisan of the texts reviewed here: unabashed in its politically (if not historically) correct definition of diversity, and in its adherence to a left-liberal view of modern America."[39] Another reviewer, Edward J. Renehan, Jr., author of the *Kennedys at War*, charged that there was "a leftist political bias" to *The Americans* by Gerald Danzer, et al. Renehan claimed, "The book's section on HUAC (House Un-American Activities Committee), Joseph McCarthy, etc. could easily have been written by Paul Robeson [noted Communist of the period]."[40] Ravitch reported that Jeffery Mirel, Associate Dean for Academic Affairs at the University of Michigan found the *American Odyssey* to have:

> a "deeply pessimistic" view, in which the nation's failures consistently out weight its commitment to its ideals ... Mirel concludes that "it is difficult to judge a book as even-handed and fair that devotes so much time to violations of people's civil liberties [in the U. S.] ... but does not even mention the millions of deaths under Soviet Communism".[41]

In summary, the image of the Republican Party as protector of traditional American values continued into the 2012 campaign. The period from the 1980s to the present day has been marked by attempts to counter negative interpretations and emphasis in writing American history. Republicans wanted a celebratory history that promoted patriotic emotions in contrast to histories that focused on enslaved Africans, the genocide and deculturalization of Native Americans, the injustices of some wars (such as the Mexican, Spanish American, and Vietnam Wars), lynchings and segregation, oppression of cultural and linguistic minorities, and violations of civil rights.

Republicans: Pro-Life, Abstinence, and Creationism

Since Republican Ronald Reagan's 1980 election, religious conservatives have been an important constituency of the Republican Party. The efforts of these religiously oriented Republicans impacted school policies particularly regarding choice plans, home schooling, school prayer, abstinence-sex education, and abortion counseling in schools.

How did these issues become part of the Republican education agenda? The answer is wrapped up in a combination of racial and religious politics. In the 1970s and 1980s, Republican leaders tried to break the attachment of Southern White and Northern White ethnic groups to the Democratic Party. During the early 1970s, President Richard Nixon consciously supported affirmative action policies as a method of dividing the Democratic coalition of Northern White union members, White ethnic groups, and minority groups. Democrats contributed to their loss of these groups by supporting affirmative-action hiring as opposed to race-neutral hiring. The result was a major realignment of parties, with many northern urban Whites flocking to the Republican camp.[42]

Also, President Nixon hoped to win over traditional Southern White Democrats by opposing school integration by the forced busing of students. The traditional Democratic Southern power structure was built around racist policies, including the segregation of public schools. Many Whites were alienated from the national Democratic Party because of its support of civil rights and joined the Republican Party. In addition, many Southern Blacks, who had traditionally viewed the Republican Party as the party of Lincoln, joined the Democratic Party. Underlying these racial politics were religious politics.[43]

Republicans hoped to recruit Christian voters who were upset by U.S. Supreme Court rulings in the 1960s and 1970s prohibiting officially conducted school prayers and Bible reading, and legalizing abortion. As a result of these decisions, many Evangelical Christians declared the public school system an enemy of Christianity and began sending their children to newly created private Christian academies. There were three important U.S. Supreme Court decisions that galvanized some religious groups into political action. The first was the 1962 U.S. Supreme Court case *Engel v. Vitale*, which denied the official use of prayer in public schools. Since the founding of common schools in the early 19th century, many public schools opened with a prayer and reading from the Protestant Bible. The 1962 decision denied the right of a public school system to conduct official prayer services within school buildings during regular school hours. The second decision was *Abington School District v. Schempp* involving a Pennsylvania law permitting the reading of ten verses from the Bible at the opening of each public school day. Again, the U.S. Supreme Court ruled that this violated the prohibition against government support of religion. Religious texts could be read, the Court argued, as part of an academic course, such as literature or history.[44] As anger swelled over the school prayer and Bible reading decisions, the U.S. Supreme Court added more fuel to the fire with the 1973 decision in *Roe v. Wade* legalizing abortion.

Fears of racial integration and godless classrooms resulted in the rapid growth of private Christian schools. Like Catholic parents, who thought it unfair to be taxed for support of public schools while they were paying tuition for religious schools, Evangelicals demanded government support of private schools. Initiating a "school choice" movement, Evangelicals argued that state and federal governments should provide financial assistance so that parents could make a choice for their children between public and private schools.[45]

Ralph Reed, a founder of the Christian Coalition and its first executive director, claimed the final straw for Evangelicals Christians was in the late 1970s when the head of the Internal Revenue Service (IRS) in the Democratic Carter administration required Christian schools to prove that they were not established to preserve segregation. During the early 1970s, there were rumblings that many of the Christian academies in the South were created as havens for White students fleeing integration. In Reed's words, "More than any other single episode, the IRS move against Christian schools sparked the explosion of the movement that would become known as the religious right."[46] "In this greater moral context," Reed announced, "faith as a political force is not undemocratic; it is the very essence of democracy."[47]

The affiliation of the religious right with the Republican Party was explained in a 1996 interview with James Pinkerton, an advisor to the Reagan and Bush administrations and author of *What Comes Next: The End of Big Government—And the New Paradigm Ahead*. In response to a question about divisions within the Republican Party, Pinkerton replied:

> Thirty years ago, Kevin Phillips, Pat Buchanan, and people like that were strategizing that we, the Republicans, win over all the southern Fundamentalists and all northern urban Catholics, and we'll build a new American majority party. And that sort of has happened. We won over a lot of urban Catholics and the South is now Republican.[48]

Also, William Kristol, editor of the conservative *Weekly Standard,* claimed, "The Republicans made the right bet demographically to bet against Episcopalians, Methodists, and Presbyterians, and with Evangelicals."[49]

The result was a Republican Party divided between those who were primarily interested in issues regarding abortion, morality, culture, and schools and those who were primarily interested in economic issues. From the perspective of religiously oriented Republicans, moderate Republicans were concerned with protecting the interests of big business. Reed wanted the Republican Party to become "the party of Main Street, not Wall Street." He went on to claim that "the real battle for the soul of our nation is not fought primarily over the gross national product and the prime interest rate, but over virtues, values, and the culture."[50] Echoing Reed, the political-religious leader Pat Buchanan rejected moderate Republican ties to business and, parodying Calvin Coolidge, said, "The business of America is not business."[51]

One leader of the so-called "electronic church," Jerry Falwell, took the concerns of the religiously oriented conservatives directly to the 1980 Republican presidential candidate, Ronald Reagan. Falwell's television program, "Old-Time Gospel Hour," was seen in more than 12 million homes in the U.S. In 1979, before meeting with Reagan, Falwell attended a lunch sponsored by The Heritage Foundation. Its director, Paul Weyrich, told him there was a "moral majority" waiting for a call to political action. Falwell jumped at the phrase and named his group the Moral Majority. Under Falwell's leadership, the organization held rallies around the country supporting the legalization of school prayer, school choice, and abolition of abortion. Within a space of two years, the Moral Majority had 2 million members and was raising $10 million annually.[52]

The wedding between Ronald Reagan and the Moral Majority occurred shortly after the 1980 Republican convention when Reagan was asked to address 20,000 Evangelicals at a rally in Dallas. Reagan told the group, "I know that you cannot endorse me [because of the tax-exempt status of the Moral Majority], but I endorse you and everything you do."[53] Giving hope to Evangelicals opposed to evolutionary theory, Reagan expressed doubts about the plausibility of Darwinian ideas. After the 1980 election, Reagan supported the religious right's agenda by endorsing legislation for a tuition tax credit to allow parents to choose between public and private schools and by promising to support a school prayer amendment to the U.S. Constitution. After 1980, school choice and school prayer became a standard fixture in Republican platforms.

By 1996, the political power of Evangelical Christians was mainly expressed through the Christian Coalition. For instance, Republican presidential candidate Bob Dole wanted to focus on an economic agenda while avoiding a strong stand against abortion, but the Christian Coalition threatened to disrupt the 1996 Convention unless the Party platform opposed abortion. Consequently, the committee writing the Republican platform capitulated to the religious right by including the following plank in the 1996 Republican Party platform: "The unborn has a fundamental individual right to life which cannot be infringed. We support a human life amendment to the Constitution and we endorse legislation to make clear that the Fourteenth Amendment's protections apply to unborn children."[54]

Compassionate Conservatism and No Child Left Behind

An important aspect of Republican ideology is that poverty is the result of the failure of individual character in contrast to claims that it results from the U.S. economic system. In recent years, Republican President George W. Bush called this argument about poverty "compassionate conservatism," which he believed was embedded in the landmark legislation No Child Left Behind Act of 2001. "Compassionate conservatism," President Bush asserted, "places great hope and confidence in public education. Our economy depends on higher and higher skills, requiring every American to have the basic tools of learning. Every public school should be the path of upward mobility."[55]

Briefly stated, compassionate conservatism—an ideology held by many conservative Christians—assumes that in most cases poverty, crime, and problems facing a democratic society are a result of a failure in personal character and values. Consequently, direct charity or government welfare doesn't solve the problem; in fact, it might reinforce negative character traits. The solution is providing the conditions by which people can help themselves. Self-help, compassionate conservatives believe, will result in a transformation of character and the acquisition of positive values. This character transformation is aided by exposure to religious values. Therefore, the imposed discipline of educational standards and testing is to help students, according to compassionate conservatives, to develop the character traits of self-discipline and hard work. Aiding in this process are character education, student-initiated school prayer, and exposure to religious values.

The importance of values was emphasized by George W. Bush when, as Governor of Texas, he wrote that:

Dream and the Nightmare by Myron Magnet crystallized for me the impact the failed culture of the sixties had on our values and society. It helped create dependency on government, undermine family and eroded values which had stood the test of time and which are critical if we want a decent and hopeful tomorrow for every single American.[56]

Myron Magnet was editor of the ultraconservative Manhattan Institute's *City Journal* and former member of the editorial board of *Fortune* magazine. He considers the 1960s and early 1970s the cultural watershed of American history. During this period, American values, he argued, deteriorated as a result of a cultural revolution led "by an elite of opinion makers, policymakers, and mythmakers—lawyers, judges, professors, political staffers, journalists, writers, TV and movie honchos, clergymen—and it was overwhelmingly a liberal, left-of-center elite."[57] Out of this cultural revolution, according to Magnet, emerged a whole host of programs, including the War on Poverty, court-ordered busing, affirmative action, drug treatment programs, and the political correctness movement at colleges.

Most important, Magnet argued, the cultural revolution overturned the traditional American values that supported hard work and family life as the basis for economic success and good living. The new values were represented by two "epochal" expressions. The first was the sexual revolution, which Magnet felt resulted in increased divorce, illegitimacy, and female-headed families. The second was the 1960s counter-culture that rejected the American economic system and its emphasis on hard work.

Basic to Magnet's argument was a belief that values determine the economic and social systems in contrast to the assumption that social and economic systems determine values. In other words, Magnet believed that the major Democratic error was trying to eliminate poverty by changing the economic system rather than changing the values of the poor. Magnet presented the following argument:

On the grandest level, if you believe that human choices and actions, rather than blind, impersonal forces, determine the shape of history, then the ideas and visions impelling the human actors become crucial causes of the reality that unfolds. Men don't simply have their environment handed to them from on high; they collectively make and remake it from the cultural and material resources that lie ready at hand. And great men augment those resources by inventing new techniques and new ideas.[58]

Magnet argued that American society advanced because of the Protestant values that promoted a free economy. Citing Max Weber, Magnet identified these values as individualism, hard work, and a belief that success is a sign of God's blessing.

Other conservatives echoed Magnet's sentiments. Pat Buchanan, the conservative political commentator and 2000 presidential candidate for the Reform Party, provided the following description of these beliefs:

> Among the social conservatives [of the Republican Party] resides the Religious Right to whom the expulsion of God from the classroom, the rise of the drug culture, and the "sexual revolution" are unmistakable symptoms of cultural decadence and national decline.[59]

Also, Bush and other religiously oriented Republicans were influenced by the work of University of Texas Journalism Professor Marvin Olasky. In his office on the Austin campus, located only a short distance from the Texas state capitol building where George W. Bush worked as the state's governor, Olasky professed the need for a rebirth of American compassion. As editor of the weekly news magazine *Christian* and as author of two important books, *The Tragedy of American Compassion* and *Renewing American Compassion: How Compassion for the Needy Can Turn Ordinary Citizens into Heroes*, Olasky blamed government welfare programs for worsening the moral conditions of the poor and, as a result, perpetuating poverty in the U.S.[60] Olasky's answer to helping the poor was returning welfare programs to faith-based organizations.

Influenced by Olasky's *Renewing American Compassion*, Bush proposed during his 2000 campaign, and later as President, that faith-based organizations be allowed to compete for federal funds. Regarding education, Bush proposed funding after-school activities operated by faith-based organizations. In reference to federal after-school programs of the 21st Century Community Learning Centers program originally created during the Clinton years, Bush suggested:

> introduc[ing] legislation to open 100 percent of the 21st Century programs funding to competitive bidding ... [to] allow youth development groups, local charities, churches, synagogues, mosques and other community and faith-based organizations to compete for these federal funds on an equal footing with schools.[61]

Federal programs operated by faith-based groups, according to Olasky and other compassionate conservatives, ensured the teaching of traditional moral values to America's poor. To Olasky, humans were basically sinful, and their inherent sinfulness must be curbed by moral instruction. The danger of providing welfare funds without demanding work in return, he argued, was that humans could easily slip into a depraved condition. Olasky maintained that in "orthodox Christian anthropology ... man's sinful nature leads toward indolence, and that an impoverished person given a dole without obligation is likely to descend into pauperism."[62]

Reforming the government welfare system was fruitless, according to Olasky, because constitutional restrictions did not allow bureaucrats to teach religious values. The only hope, he argued, was to replace government programs with charities operated by faith-based organizations. Olasky supported his argument with a historical survey of private charities that included the exhortation of 17th-century Puritan divine Cotton Mather: "Don't nourish [the idle] and harden'em in that, but find employment for them. Find'em work; set'em to work; keep'em to work."[63]

Olasky maintained there were beneficial results from a direct relationship between the giver and receiver as opposed to a relationship between a faceless government bureaucracy and a receiver. Giving, he declared, was a moral act. Personal charity benefited the giver through engagement with the suffering of others. The engagement with suffering supposedly strengthened the religious faith of the giver which, in turn, provided a model of religious values for the recipient. Consequently, replacing government-operated welfare programs with faith-based and personal charity, according to Olasky, strengthened the general moral values of society while providing the poor with a real means of escaping poverty. Regarding the Christian definition of compassion, Olasky stated that, "The word points to personal involvement with the needy, suffering with them, not just giving to them. 'Suffering with' means adopting hard-to-place babies, providing shelter to women undergoing crisis ... working one-on-one with a single mother."[64]

Compassionate conservatism is based on the importance of ideas as they affect values and character in determining social conditions. Therefore, control of schools and media is important. Pat Buchanan quotes Giuseppe Mazzini: "Ideas rule the world and its events. A revolution is a passage of an idea from theory to practice. Whatever men say, material interests never caused and never will cause a revolution."[65] Agreeing with Buchanan, William Bennett, who served nine years in public office as head of the National Endowment for the Humanities, as U.S. Secretary of Education under Ronald Reagan, and the first drug czar under George H. W. Bush, stated that:

> I have come to the conclusion that the issues surrounding the culture and our values are the most important ones ... They are at the heart of our resolution of the knottiest problems of public policy, whether the subject be education, art, race relations, drugs, crime, or raising children.[66]

For Bennett, the solution to public problems was the teaching of morality along with his emphasis on Western cultural values. To support the conviction that an acceptance of Christ and Christian morality are necessary for maintaining democracy, Bennett quoted George Washington's farewell address: "Of all the dispositions and habits which lead to political prosperity, religion and morality are indispensable supports ... And let us with caution indulge the supposition that morality can be maintained without religion."[67] Using similar language, Ralph Reed argued that democracy depends on citizens and their government showing allegiance to God. "In this greater moral context," Reed wrote, "faith as a political force is not undemocratic; it is the very essence of democracy."[68]

In contrast, Michael Lind, a former conservative and now a critic of the right, argued that religious right Republicans, such as Buchanan and Olasky, launched a cultural war against public schools as a method of diverting "the wrath of wage-earning populist voters from Wall Street and corporate America to other targets: the universities, the media, racial minorities, homosexuals, immigrants."[69] In fact, Lind referred to conservative claims of a crisis in public education as their "second great policy hoax," resulting in many Americans being persuaded that the schools are failing the nation.[70]

Believing in the overriding importance of Christian morality and culture for solving social problems and maintaining democracy, the religiously oriented conservatives support school prayer, school choice, abolition of secular humanism in public schools, censorship of textbooks and books in school libraries, restricting sex education to teaching abstinence, and ending school-based abortion counseling and family planning.

Compassionate Conservatives and No Child Left Behind

How were the concerns of compassionate conservatives expressed in No Child Left Behind? First, No Child Left Behind supported public funding of faith-based organizations; something dear to the hearts of compassionate conservatives. In its many sections, No Child Left Behind allowed funding of faith-based organizations. In July, 2004, the U.S. Department of Education issued a pamphlet describing the relationship between No Child Left Behind and faith-based organizations. The pamphlet asserted:

> With No Child Left Behind, schools and religious organizations can become even more powerful allies in the effort to ensure that all children— regardless of their race, family income or the language spoken in their homes—receive a high-quality education.[71]

The pamphlet described the following opportunities for faith-based organizations to participate in No Child Left Behind:

> Faith-based organizations can receive funds to provide tutoring and other academic enrichment services for eligible low-income students. Religious organizations can become supplemental educational services providers by applying to states and then working with districts to provide services directly to students in reading language arts and mathematics.[72]

In addition to becoming supplemental educational services providers, faith-based groups can receive grants from a range of other programs that provide extra academic help.

Bush's Secretary of Education Rod Paige was a fan of government funding of faith-based organizations. Standing in front of a poster proclaiming "Compassion in Action" at the 11th Regional White House Conference on Faith-Based and Community Initiatives, Secretary Paige declared:

> With a stroke of a pen, the President signaled that this Administration will knock down any barrier, will do whatever it takes to get people of faith and goodwill involved in helping solve some of the problems in our society.[73]

When John Porter was appointed U.S. Department of Education's Director of Faith-Based and Community Initiatives, Secretary Paige used the language of compassionate conservatism to describe him:

> John Porter is a leader in our nation's army of compassion. Some of the most successful, uplifting and effective programs to help children are run by faith-based and community organizations. We plan to utilize the hundreds of faith-based and community soldiers around the country to ensure that every child of every religion, race and ethnicity gets the best education America can offer them, and John will help guide our efforts.[74]

Since these religiously oriented Republicans were associating poverty with a failure in individual character and values, it was logical that No Child Left Behind would contain programs for character education. The character education and religious sections of No Child Left Behind directly support compassionate conservative ideology.

No Child Left Behind links character education to democracy and a free-market economy. The legislation's "Section 2345: Cooperative Civic Education and Economic Education" supports research to determine the:

> effects of educational programs on students' development of the knowledge, skills, and *traits of character essential* for the preservation and *improvement of constitutional democracy*; and . . . effective participation in, and the preservation and improvement of, *an efficient market economy* [author's emphasis].[75]

Character education is also included in drug and violence prevention programs funded by the legislation.[76]

The central character education part of No Child Left Behind is "Section 5431: Partnerships in Character Education Program" which supports "the design and implementation of character education programs that . . . are able to be integrated into classroom instruction and to be consistent with State academic content standards."[77] This section of the legislation even listed possible elements of character education instruction; this may be the first time in history where federal legislation actually identified elements of character considered important for the functioning of American society. The legislation provides the following examples:

(A) Caring.
(B) Civic virtue and citizenship.
(C) Justice and fairness.
(D) Respect.
(E) Responsibility.
(F) Trustworthiness.
(G) Giving.[78]

In 2002, the U.S. Department of Education began funding applications for character education programs under the No Child Left Behind Act. U.S. Secretary of Education Rod Paige announced in 2003, "We have invested nearly $24 million in character education in FY 2003 because we believe that building strong character is as essential as reading, math and science."[79] However, the results were disappointing. In 2007, the U.S Secretary of Education released a report which, according to *Education Week* reporter Debra Viadero, "After reviewing the research on 41 programs aimed at instilling character in students, the U.S. Department of Education gave 'positive' ratings to just two of them and rated seven more as 'potentially positive'."[80]

No Child Left Behind and School Prayer

The No Child Left Behind legislation deals directly with an issue dear to the hearts of many religiously oriented Republicans, namely school prayer. The legislation's "Section 9524: School Prayer" commands:

> The Secretary [U.S. Secretary of Education] shall provide and revise guidance, not later than September 1, 2002, and of every second year thereafter, to State educational agencies, local educational agencies, and the public on *constitutionally protected prayer* in public elementary schools and secondary schools, including making the guidance available on the Internet.[81]

This section of the legislation was in response to the failure to add an amendment to the U.S. Constitution allowing for school prayer and concerns about the supposed emphasis on secular humanism in public schools. The religious right defines secular humanism as dependence on human reason in contrast to faith in God as a guide for ethical decisions. Without God in the school, the religious right believes, the school becomes a place for teaching secular humanism. An important court case involving secular humanism began in 1983 in the schools of Hawkins County, Tennessee, when a local parent expressed concern about a new series of readers published by Holt, Rinehart, and Winston. According to the complaint, the books were filled with "minorities, foreigners, environmentalism, women in nontraditional roles, and open-ended value judgments without clear right and wrong answers."[82] The case attracted the attention of a wide variety of religious groups opposed to the teaching of secular humanism, such as Phyllis Schlafly's Eagle Forum, the National Association of Christian Educators, Citizens for Excellence in Education, Concerned Women for America, Pat Robertson's National Legal Foundation, and the American Family Association. In opposition to these groups was the liberal organization People for the American Way.

Criticism of the textbooks included a wide range of topics under the banner of secular humanism. Believing that unregulated capitalism was God's will, critics objected to suggestions of environmentalism because it led to government intervention in the economy. Protestors objected to teaching religious tolerance because it suggested that other religions were equal in value to Christianity. The teaching of international cooperation, Evangelicals argued, could lead to world government, which would mean the reign, in their eyes, of the antichrist. They also objected to stories that suggested humane treatment of animals and vegetarianism because God created animals for human use and exploitation. Evangelicals particularly objected to any story suggesting that hunting was wrong. Also, they felt that stories suggesting the depletion of resources and the extinction of species were denying God's promise to meet all human needs. Men and women portrayed in nontraditional roles would, according to protestors, destroy the traditional Christian family in which wives remained at home raising their children. For this reason, they opposed anything that smacked of feminism.[83]

After four years of litigation, the Sixth Circuit Court of Appeals ruled that public schools did not have to accommodate religious objections to the Holt, Rinehart, and Winston readers. A previous lower court ruling suggested that religious objections to the books could be accommodated by assigning different texts or by teaching reading at home. The final ruling enhanced the power of school boards by requiring children attending public schools to read the books selected by school officials.[84]

In 1987, the National Legal Foundation, affiliated with Pat Robertson's Christian Broadcasting Network, provided support for an Alabama case against public schools teaching secular humanism. Robertson used his television show, "The 700 Club," to publicize the case as a Christian battle against the antireligious tenets of secular humanism. People for the American Way and the American Civil Liberties Union provided legal opposition to the work of the National Legal Foundation. The case received a great deal of attention when Robertson announced his candidacy for the presidency in 1988.[85]

The plaintiffs charged that 45 textbooks approved for Alabama schools taught secular humanism. Supporting their case was a consent decree signed by Alabama's

Governor George Wallace stating that the religion of secular humanism should be excluded from Alabama schools. On The 700 Club, Robertson quoted former Alabama Governor and pro-segregationist George Wallace, "I don't want to teach ungodly humanism in the schools where I'm governor." In turn, Robertson declared that taking secular humanism out of the schools was an issue of "religious freedom."[86]

The primary legal problem for the plaintiffs was proving that secular humanism was a religion. Again, the issue was about textbooks teaching children that they could make their own moral decisions without relying on the authority of the Word of God. In a lower court decision, religious conservative Judge Brevard Hand ruled that secular humanism was indeed a religion and that the use of books espousing secular humanism should be removed from the schools. This decision was reversed by the Eleventh Circuit Court of Appeals, which ruled that the books did not violate the First Amendment: "Rather the message conveyed is one of a governmental attempt to instill in Alabama public school children such values as independent thought, tolerance of diverse views, self-respect, maturity, self-reliance, and logical decision-making. This is an entirely appropriate secular effect."[87]

In 1994, after failing to counter secular humanism and achieve a school prayer amendment, the Christian Coalition decided to make what Reed called a "seismic shift" in strategy. Rather than campaigning for school prayer, the decision was made to adopt Robertson's language and support an amendment for religious freedom. Reed argued that an emphasis on religious freedom as opposed to the narrower issue of school prayer would appeal to a broader religious audience. The religious freedom amendment would guarantee the right of religious expression to all people in all public settings.[88] In 1996, reflecting what was now becoming a compromise position about school prayer, Haley Barbour, Chairman of the National Republican Committee, stated that the Republican Party supported the "right to voluntary prayer in schools ... whether through a constitutional amendment or through legislation, or a combination of both."[89]

Leaders of the Christian Coalition hoped that a religious-freedom amendment would protect the rights of students to express their religious beliefs in the classroom. For example, it was believed that a student should have the right to support creationism over evolutionary theory in science classes. In supporting the religious-freedom amendment, Reed described the case of a Tennessee high school student, Brittney Settle, who was failed for turning in an essay on the life of Jesus Christ. Without citing the details of the case, Reed claimed that a federal court upheld the right of the school to flunk the student for her religious beliefs. In reaction to the case, Reed stated, "A religious freedom amendment would protect her, along with unbelieving students who are nervous about being compelled to participate in mandatory religious exercises in public schools."[90]

Republican representatives Newt Gingrich and Dick Armey promised the Christian Coalition that for its support of Republican candidates they would introduce a proposal for inclusion of religious freedom in the First Amendment. The proposed changes to the First Amendment would "protect religious freedom, including the right of students in public schools to pray without government sponsorship or compulsion." In addition, the changes would prohibit state and federal governments from denying anyone "equal access to a benefit, or otherwise discriminate against any person, on account of religious belief, expression, or exercise."[91]

During the hearings, Republican representative Henry Hyde, the head of the House Judiciary Committee, complained that public school teachers often discriminated against Christians by denying reports and essays on Jesus Christ. "Public school teachers, who accept reports on witches," Hyde explained, "[and] forbid students from writing reports on Jesus. This is madness."[92] One cynical critic, David Ramage, Jr., President Emeritus of the McCormick Theological Seminary, accused the Christian Coalition of wanting to rush the amendments through the House of Representatives so that House members' positions could be included in their fall voting guide. Voting "no" on the religious-freedom changes, Ramage suggested, would be listed in the Christian Coalition's voter guide as "a vote against religious freedom" or a "vote against God."[93]

Unable to achieve an amendment to the U.S. Constitution, No Child Left Behind was seen as an opportunity to protect religious freedom. The school prayer section of No Child Left Behind mandated the protection of religious freedom in public schools. The legislation required the U.S. Secretary of Education to issue guidance for protecting constitutionally approved prayer. Dated February 7, 2003, the U.S. Department of Education guide reminded local education agencies that they must report that their schools have "no policy that prevents, or otherwise denies participation in, constitutionally protected prayer in public schools as set forth in this guidance."[94] The guidelines state, although the Constitution forbids public school officials from directing or favoring prayer, students do not "shed their constitutional rights to freedom of speech or expression at the schoolhouse gate," and the Supreme Court has made clear that "private religious speech, far from being a First Amendment orphan, is as fully protected under the Free Speech Clause as secular private expression." Moreover, not all religious speech that takes place in the public schools or at school-sponsored events is governmental speech. For example, "nothing in the Constitution ... prohibits any public school student from voluntarily praying at any time before, during, or after the school day," and students may pray with fellow students during the school day on the same terms and conditions that they may engage in other conversation or speech. Likewise, local school authorities possess substantial discretion to impose rules of order and pedagogical restrictions on student activities, but they may not structure or administer such rules to discriminate against student prayer or religious speech.[95]

The 2008 Republican platform restated the No Child Left Behind support of religious freedom in public schools: "We will energetically assert the right of students to engage in voluntary prayer in schools and to have equal access to school facilities for religious purposes."[96] The 2012 Republican platform reiterated its support of school prayer and public display of religious messages:

> We support the public display of the Ten Commandments as a reflection of our history and of our country's Judeo-Christian heritage, and we affirm the right of students to engage in prayer at public school events in public schools and to have equal access to public schools and other public facilities to accommodate religious freedom in the public square.[97]

Pornography, Family Planning, and Traditional Marriage

Conservative religious values concerning sexuality also appear in No Child Left Behind and in the 2012 Republican platform. The 2012 platform restated Republican opposition to gay marriage:

> We reaffirm our support for a Constitutional amendment defining marriage as the union of one man and one woman. We applaud the citizens of the majority of States which have enshrined in their constitutions the traditional concept of marriage, and we support the campaigns underway in several other States to do so.[98]

Personal sexual values are a central concern for religiously oriented Republicans. Also, among some religious groups, thinking and imagining sexual activities is the same as engaging in them. Consequently, some Republicans believe that control of pornography and sex education programs that teach abstinence from sexual activity are essential for building character traits that value hard work, personal advancement, and a democratic society. The concern with sexuality is based on the principle that ideas, as opposed to material conditions, determine the course of civilization. Reflecting on his experience as a student in a Roman Catholic high school where the Jesuit teachers made the possession of pornography a reason for expulsion, Republican Pat Buchanan explains:

> Far greater harm has come, not only to souls but to nations, from polluted books and evil ideas—racism, militarism, Nazism, Communism—than has ever come from polluted streams or rotten food. With the Bible [the Jesuit teachers] taught that it is not what goes in the stomach that "defiles a man, but what comes out of his mouth".[99]

Republicans reacted swiftly when gay/lesbian marriage became an issue in the early 21st century. The 2004 Republican platform called for a Constitutional Amendment that would make gay/lesbian marriages illegal:

> We strongly support President Bush's call for a Constitutional amendment that fully protects marriage . . . We believe, and the social science confirms, that the well-being of children is best accomplished in the environment of the home, nurtured by their mother and father anchored by the bonds of marriage.[100]

The 2008 Republican platform devoted a whole section to "Preserving Traditional Marriage" which opened:

> Because our children's future is best preserved within the traditional understanding of marriage, we call for a constitutional amendment that fully protects marriage as a union of a man and a woman . . . In the absence of a national amendment, we support the right of the people of the various states to affirm traditional marriage through state initiatives.[101]

An attempt to curb the social acceptance of gays and lesbians appeared in a section of No Child Left Behind called "Boy Scouts of America Equal Access Act." This section of the legislation was in response to a decision in the 1990s by the Boy Scouts to deny membership to homosexuals. In 2000, the U.S. Supreme Court ruled in *Boy Scouts of America v. Dale* that the Boy Scouts was a private association and had the right to set its own standards for membership and leadership. As a result, school districts across the country banned the Boy Scouts from using school facilities because they discriminated against homosexuals. In the "Boy Scouts of America Equal Access Act" of No Child Left Behind, public schools receiving funds under the legislation are prohibited from denying Boy Scouts use of school facilities. The legislation states:

> Notwithstanding any other provision of law, no public elementary school, public secondary school, local educational agency, or State educational agency that has a designated open forum or a limited public forum and that receives funds made available through the Department shall deny equal access or a fair opportunity to meet to, or discriminate against, any group officially affiliated with the Boy Scouts of America.[102]

Religious conservatives were also concerned about pornography on the World Wide Web and television. In its effort to remove pornography or, as it is called, cyberporn, from the World Wide Web, the Christian Coalition sought the aid of Democrats after Massachusetts Democratic Representative Edward Markey introduced a bill requiring television manufacturers to install "v-chips" to allow parents to block programs with too much violence.[103] Working with a group of Democrats and Republicans, the Christian Coalition claimed a major responsibility for the writing of the 1995 Telecommunications Act requiring censorship of cyberporn and v-chips. The work on the telecommunications bill demonstrated that the Christian Coalition could influence both political parties. Reed argued that the relationship between Evangelical Christians and the Republican Party is simply strategic. "The two are not one and the same," he stated. "Indeed, the partnership between the profamily movement and the GOP is less a romance than a shotgun wedding."[104]

No Child Left Behind included these concerns in "Title II–Preparing, Training and Recruiting High Quality Teachers and Principals." Title II requires schools to have "a policy of Internet safety for minors ... that protects against access through such computers to visual depictions that are—(i) obscene; (ii) child pornography; or (iii) harmful to minors."[105]

No Child Left Behind also contains prohibitions against using any money granted on the legislation that might promote birth control or homosexuality. Section 9526: General prohibitions specifically states that:

> None of the funds authorized under this Act shall be used ... to develop or distribute materials, or operate programs or courses of instruction directed at youth, that are designed to promote or encourage sexual activity, whether homosexual or heterosexual.[106]

Also, funds cannot be used "to distribute or to aid in the distribution by any organization of *legally* obscene materials to minors on school grounds [author's emphasis]."[107] And, No Child Left Behind promotes abstinence education and bans teaching about birth control by prohibiting funds for "sex education or HIV-prevention education in schools unless that instruction is age appropriate and includes the health benefits of abstinence; or ... to operate a program of contraceptive distribution in schools."[108]

Evolution Versus Creationism

In 2013, national science standards were released with a concern that their adoption would be thwarted by resistance to theories of evolution and climate change. *Education Week* reported:

> It remains to be seen whether the standards' handling of climate-change education and evolution will make adoption in certain states more politically difficult. The standards make clear that evolution is fundamental to understanding the life sciences. They also call for teaching about climate change and describe human activities as "major factors".[109]

As of 2011, only seven states along with the District of Columbia provided a "comprehensive treatment of human evolution."[110] In addition, it was reported that 80 percent of Americans believe God created humans in their present form or guided the process of evolution.[111] These figures suggest that teaching evolution in schools will remain a contentious subject.

Concerns about teaching evolution was highlighted in 2001 when the Kansas State Board of Education voted to reinstate the theory of evolution in the state's science curriculum after a bitter struggle by creationists to have it removed. For Christian fundamentalists, evolutionary theory contradicts the Word of God as literally interpreted from the Bible regarding the creation of humans. Creationists believe that a divine being created humans and other species. They say that because evolution cannot be observed or replicated in a laboratory, there is no evidence that it actually occurred. In the Kansas controversy the "big bang" theory, which contends that the universe was born from a vast explosion, had also been dropped from the curriculum.

The Kansas struggle over the place of evolution in the curriculum echoed the famous 1920s' Scopes trial, in which high school biology teacher John T. Scopes was accused of violating Tennessee's Butler Act, which forbade the teaching of evolutionary theory. Scopes was convicted of violating the law, but the verdict was later reversed on technical grounds by the state supreme court. However, the Butler Act remained in effect until 1967. Other states also have recently been embroiled in the evolution controversy. In Alabama, New Mexico, and Nebraska, laws and administrative actions require that evolution be presented as theory that it is merely one possible explanation. The Texas, Ohio, Washington, New Hampshire, and Tennessee legislatures defeated similar bills, including the requirement that teachers also present evidence to disprove the theory. Alabama now requires that biology textbooks contain a sticker calling evolution "a controversial theory some scientists present as a scientific explanation for the origin of living things." The sticker also warns students that "No one was present when life first appeared on earth. Therefore, any statement about life's origins should be considered as theory, not fact."[112]

For some, evolutionary theory is more than just a scientific dispute—it goes to the heart of the debate about values. Mark Looy of Answers in Genesis, a creationist group, said:

> Students in public schools are being taught that evolution is a fact, that they're just products of survival of the fittest. There's not meaning in life if we're just animals in a struggle for survival. It creates a sense of purposelessness and hopelessness, which I think leads to things like pain, murder and suicide.[113]

The Kansas controversy over teaching evolutionary theory began when the Kansas State Board of Education deleted it from the state's science curriculum.

Although the action did not forbid schools from teaching the subject, it did remove the topic from the state's science tests. This meant that schools could ignore the theory while teaching biology without any resulting harm to students required to take the state's examinations. The issue originally arose in 1998, when the state board appointed a group of scientists to develop state standards for teaching science. When the standards were reviewed by the board, Steve Abrams, a conservative member of the board and former chairman of the state Republican Party, declared it was "not good science to teach evolution as fact."[114] With the help of other religious fundamentalists, he rewrote the standards by deleting two pages on evolution while retaining a section on "micro-evolution" that dealt with genetic changes and natural selection within a species. In addition, Abrams added to the state standards, "The design and complexity of the design of the cosmos requires [sic] an intelligent designer."[115] After much debate, the board adopted the rewritten standards by a vote of 6 to 4.

The decision of the Kansas State Board of Education created a political firestorm. Kansas Governor Bill Graves declared the new science standards "terrible" and "tragic," resulting in a split in the state's Republican Party, with Governor Graves supporting the moderate Republicans who favored the teaching of evolution and Kansas' Republican Senator Sam Brownback supporting conservatives who opposed it.[116]

Groups outside of Kansas became embroiled in the political dispute. People for the American Way, a group organized for the specific purpose of countering the political actions of the religiously oriented conservatives, brought Ed Asner to the University of Kansas to re-enact the Scopes trial. Phillip Johnson, a University of California Law Professor, donated money to conservative candidates who espoused his belief in the "intelligent design" theory.[117]

Conservative candidates were defeated in the election. On February 14, 2001, the Kansas State Board of Education reversed its previous decision on evolution by a vote of 7 to 3. Highlighting struggle over evolution was a warning to teachers placed in the Kansas science standards:

> Teachers should not ridicule, belittle or embarrass a student for expressing an alternative view or belief. If a student should raise a question in a natural science class that the teacher determines to be outside the domain of science, the teacher should treat the question with respect. The teacher should explain why the question is outside the domain of natural science and encourage the student to discuss the question further with his or her family and other appropriate sources.[118]

Creation Museum

In 2008, I toured the Creation Museum in Northern Kentucky.[119] The Museum directly confronts the conflict between scientists arguing that the era of dinosaurs lasted for about 160 million years and a literal reading of the Bible which places creation at a little over 4,000 years ago. The resolution is Museum displays showing humans coexisting with dinosaurs. The Museum is filled with dioramas of animatronic dinosaurs and humans. The Museum website describes: "The Creation Museum, located seven miles west of the Cincinnati Airport, presents a 'walk through history'." Designed by a former Universal Studios exhibit director, this state-of-the-art 70,000 square foot museum brings the pages of the Bible to life. It is described as:

> A fully engaging, sensory experience for guests. Murals and realistic scenery, computer-generated visual effects, over fifty exotic animals, life-sized people and dinosaur animatronics, and a special-effects theater complete with misty sea breezes and rumbling seats. These are just some of the impressive exhibits that everyone in your family will enjoy.[120]

How do you reconcile scientific evidence with a literal interpretation of the Bible dates? Throughout the museum are signs showing differences in interpretations based on reason and faith: "Reason is human and faith is a relationship with God. Humans err and therefore reason errs while faith links a person to the truth of God."

The effects of teaching evolutionary theory are depicted in two Creation Museum photos. In one photo a woman is shown in despair surrounded by representations of drugs and alcohol. In the next photo, she is released from despair by rejecting evolutionary theory for creationism. Why? Because creationism teaches that she is a singular creature of God while evolutionary theory robs her of that sense of being God's special creature.

The museum shop offers curricula and schoolbooks about creationism. One diorama depicts a life-like secondary or middle school boy exclaiming, "I never heard this before in school." A life-like girl is tugging on his arm saying, "Come on. Let me show you the rest."

Conclusion: The Cross and the Flag

The Republican Party nourishes an image of itself as protector of traditional American and Christian values. This image makes it possible for Republicans to recruit voters who were offended by the 1960s' counter-culture movement and U.S. Supreme Court decisions regarding school prayer, school Bible reading, and abortion. This Republican strategy for building a new party constituency impacted the Republican education agenda. It made central to the Republican education agenda promotion in schools of patriotism, English-only, unity around traditional American cultural values, a positive-oriented American history, and America's exceptionalism as the leader of the free world. As protector of traditional American religious values, the Republican education agenda endorses abstinence education, religious freedom as a protection of school prayer, choice at public expense of religious schools, and the teaching of creationism alongside evolutionary theory in science classes.

Notes

1 Drew Westen, *The Political Brain: The Role of Emotion in Deciding the Fate of the Nation* (New York: Public Affairs, 2007), pp. 145–169.
2 2012 Republican Platform, "We Believe in America," p. 36.
3 Ibid., p. 36.
4 Ibid., p. 35.
5 Ibid., p. 37.
6 William J. Bennett, *The De-Valuing of America: The Fight for Our Culture and Our Children* (New York: Simon & Schuster, 1992), p. 170.
7 Ibid., p. 170.
8 Ibid., p. 26.
9 Lynne Cheney, "American Memory: A Report on the Humanities in the Nation's Public Schools" (Washington, DC: National Endowment for the Humanities, 1987).
10 Quoted in "Humanities Instruction Is Assailed" (September 9, 1987) *Education Week*. Retrieved from http://www.edweek.org/ew/articles/1987/09/09/07260031.h07. html?qs=Humanities+Instruction+Is+Assailed on March 2, 2008.
11 Ibid.
12 "Republican Party Platform of 1996," p. 48. Retrieved from http://www.presidency. ucsb.edu/ws/?pid=25848 on March 26, 2009.
13 Ibid., p. 37.
14 Quoted in ibid.
15 Ibid.
16 "Republican Party Platform of 2000," p. 33. Retrieved from http://www.presidency. ucsb.edu/ws/?pid=25849 on March 26, 2009.
17 Ibid., p. 33.
18 Ibid.
19 "Diane Ravitch: Curriculum Vitae."
20 Catherine Cornbleth and Dexter Waugh, *The Great Speckled Bird: Multicultural Politics and Education Policymaking* (Mahwah, NJ: Lawrence Erlbaum Associates, Inc., 1995), pp. 16–17, 68–71.
21 Ibid., pp. 93–185.
22 Arthur M. Schlesinger, Jr., *The Disuniting of America* (Knoxville, TN: Whittle Direct Books, 1991), p. 8.
23 Quoted in Caroline B. Cody, Arthur Woodward, and David L. Elliot, "Race, Ideology and the Battle Over the Curriculum," in *The New Politics of Race and Gender* (Washington, DC: Falmer Press, 1993), p. 55.
24 Quoted in Cornbleth and Waugh, *The Great Speckled Bird*, p. 85.
25 Quoted in ibid., p. 65.
26 Quoted in ibid., p. 65.
27 Quoted in ibid., p. 66.
28 "Plan to Teach U.S. History Is Said to Slight White Males," *The New York Times* (October 26, 1994), B12.
29 Carol Gluck, "Let the Debate Continue," *The New York Times* (October 26, 1994), p. 23.
30 Karen Diegmueller, "Revise History Standards, Two Panels Advise," *Education Week* (October 18, 1995), p. 11.
31 Ibid.

32 Ibid.
33 Karen Diegmueller, "History Center Shares New Set of Standards," *Education Week* (April 10, 1996), p. 1.
34 Bob Dole and Jack Kemp, *Trusting the People: The Dole-Kemp Plan to Free the Economy and Create a Better America* (New York: HarperCollins, 1996), p. 92.
35 D'Souza, "We the Slaveowners," p. 74.
36 Dinesh D'Souza, *Illiberal Education: The Politics of Race and Sex on Campus* (New York: Vintage Books, 1992); see also *The End of Racism* (New York: Free Press, 1995).
37 Ibid., p. 42.
38 Diane Ravitch, *A Consumer's Guide to High School History Textbooks* (Washington, DC: Fordham Institute, 2004).
39 Ibid., p. 33.
40 Ibid., p. 42.
41 Ibid., p. 35.
42 See Jacob Weisberg, *In Defense of Government: The Fall and Rise of Public Trust* (New York: Scribner's, 1996) and Michael Tomasky, *Left for Dead: The Life, Death and Possible Resurrection of Progressive Politics in America* (New York: Free Press, 1996).
43 Ibid.
44 See Spring, *The American School*, pp. 459–460.
45 Ibid., pp. 448–462.
46 Ralph Reed, *Active Faith: How Christians Are Changing the Soul of American Politics* (New York: Free Press, 1996), p. 105.
47 Ibid., p. 9.
48 Quoted in Jacob Weisberg, "Fear and Self-Loathing," *The New York Times* (August 19, 1996), p. 36.
49 Ibid., p. 36.
50 Reed, *Active Faith*, pp. 4, 11.
51 Patrick J. Buchanan, *Right From the Beginning* (Washington, DC: Regnery Gateway, 1990), p. 6.
52 Reed, *Active Faith*, pp. 109–111.
53 Ibid., p. 111.
54 "Republican Party Platform of 1996," p. 33.
55 George W. Bush, *On God and Country* edited by Thomas Freiling (Washington, DC: Allegiance Press, Inc, 2004), p. 122.
56 George W. Bush, Comment on the front cover of Myron Magnet, *The Dream and the Nightmare: The Sixties' Legacy to the Underclass* (San Francisco: Encounter Books, 2000).
57 Ibid., p. 20.
58 Ibid., p. 24.
59 Buchanan, *Right From the Beginning*, p. 14.
60 Marvin Olasky, *The Tragedy of American Compassion* (Wheaton, IL: Crossway Books, 1995) and *Renewing American Compassion: How Compassion for the Needy Can Turn Ordinary Citizens into Heroes* (Washington, DC: Regnery, 1997).
61 "Educational Policy Statement of Bush Campaign." Retrieved from http://www.georgebush.com on August 24, 2000.
62 Olasky, *Renewing American Compassion*, pp. 41–42.
63 Ibid., p. 36
64 Ibid., pp. 29–30.
65 Buchanan, *Right From the Beginning*, p. 14.
66 Bennett, *The De-Valuing of America*, p. 36.
67 Ibid., p. 206.
68 Ralph Reed, *Active Faith: How Christians Are Changing the Soul of American Politics* (New York: Free Press, 1996), p. 9.

69 Michael Lind, *Up From Conservatism: Why the Right Is Wrong for America* (New York: Free Press, 1996), p. 154.

70 Ibid., p. 161.

71 U.S. Department of Education, "No Child Left Behind and Faith-Based Leaders: Working Together So All Children Succeed" (Washington, DC: U.S. Government Printing Office, 2004). Retrieved from the U.S. Department of Education http://www.ed.gov/nclb/freedom/faith/leaders.pdf on January 7, 2005.

72 Ibid.

73 Roderick Paige, "White House Conference on Faith-Based and Community Initiatives." Retrieved from the U.S. Department of Education http://www.ed.gov/news/speeches/2002/10/10102002.html on March 7, 2004.

74 Press Release, "Paige Names John Porter as Director of Department's Center for Faith-Based and Community Initiatives" (May 29, 2002). Retrieved from the U.S. Department of Education http://www.ed.gov/news/pressreleases/2002/05/05292002a.html on April 10, 2003.

75 *No Child Left Behind Act of 2001, Public Law 107–110* (January 8, 2002), pp. 240–241. Retrieved from the U.S. Department of Education http://www2.ed.gov/policy/elsec/leg/esea02/107-110.pdf on April 2, 2009.

76 Ibid., p. 341.

77 Ibid., p. 393.

78 Ibid., pp. 394–395.

79 Press Release, "Character Education Grants Awarded."

80 Debra Viadero, "Proof of Positive Effect Found for Only a Few Character Programs," *Education Week* (June 20, 2007). Retrieved from http://www.edweek.org/ew/articles/2007/06/20/ on April 3, 2009.

81 *No Child Left Behind Act of 2001*, pp. 556–557.

82 Joan Delfattore, *What Johnny Shouldn't Read: Textbook Censorship in America* (New Haven, CT: Yale University Press, 1992), p. 14.

83 Ibid., pp. 36–60.

84 Ibid., pp. 61–75.

85 Ibid., pp. 76–79.

86 Ibid., p. 81.

87 Ibid., p. 87.

88 Reed, *Active Faith*, pp. 117–118.

89 Haley Barbour, *Agenda for America: A Republican Direction for the Future* (Washington, DC: Regnery, 1996), p. 159.

90 Reed, *Active Faith* ..., p. 118.

91 See Eric Schmitt, "Church Leaders Split on Plan for School Prayer Amendment," *The New York Times* (July 24, 1995), p. A16.

92 Ibid., p. A16.

93 Ibid., p. A16.

94 U.S. Department of Education, "Guidance on Constitutionally Protected Prayer in Public Elementary and Secondary Schools" (February 7, 2003). Retrieved from http://www.ed.gov/policy/gen/guid/religionandschools/prayer_guidance.html on March 7, 2003.

95 Ibid.

96 "Republican Platform of 2008," pp. 44–45.

97 2012 Republican Platform, "We Believe in America," p. 12.

98 Ibid., p. 10.

99 Buchanan, *Right From the Beginning*, p. 339.

100 "Republican Platform of 2004," p. 86.

101 "Republican Platform of 2008," p. 53.

102 *No Child Left Behind*, p. 557.

103 Reed, *Active Faith*, pp. 229–231.

104 Ibid., p. 234.

105 *No Child Left Behind*, p. 262.

106 Ibid., p. 558.

107 Ibid., p. 558.

108 Ibid., p. 558.

109 Erik W. Robelen, "Standards in Science Unveiled," *Education Week* (April 16, 2013). Retrieved from http://www.edweek.org/ew/articles/2013/04/17/28science_ep-2. h32.html?qs=evolution on May 14, 2013.

110 Jennifer Oldham, "The Evolution of Teaching Evolution," *Education* Week (February 11, 2011). Retrieved from http://www.edweek.org/ew/articles/2011/02/11/21thr_ evolution_ep.h30.html?tkn=ZOLFSueu%2FW43DYC9D6pL9qjKw0wKfBChh524& print=1 on May 14, 2013.

111 Ibid.

112 Pam Belluck, "Kansas Votes to Delete Evolution From State's Science Curriculum" (August 12, 1999). Retrieved from http://www.nytimes.com/library/on September 24, 2000.

113 Ibid.

114 Ibid.

115 Ibid.

116 Pam Belluck, "Board Decision on Evolution Roils an Election in Kansas" (July 29, 2000). Retrieved from http://www.nytimes.com/library/on September 24, 2000.

117 Ibid.

118 John W. Fountain, "Kansas Puts Evolution Back Into Public Schools" (February 15, 2001). Retrieved from http://www.nytimes.com/library/ on March 29, 2001.

119 Information about the Creation Museum can be found on its website http://www. creationmuseum.org/.

120 "Creation Museum: Prepare to Believe." Retrieved from http://www.creationmuseum. org/ on April 5, 2009.

5

GREEN AND LIBERTARIAN PARTY AGENDAS

The Green Party's 2012 call to "Repeal the No Child Left Behind Act"[1] stands in sharp contrast to proposals in the Republican and Democratic platforms and to the 2012 Libertarian Party platform's claim that: "Education is best provided by the free market, achieving greater quality, accountability and efficiency with more diversity of choice."[2] Both the Green and Libertarian Parties provide voters with important alternative education agendas to that of the two major political parties. The Green Party's education agenda is focused on preparing critical and active citizens, teaching sustainable development, maintaining democratic control of local schools, and integrating the arts into school curricula. The Libertarian Party's education agenda reflects its commitment to free-market ideas and choice by separation of school and state. The Libertarian Party would probably agree with the Green Party that No Child Left Behind and the results of Race to the Top should be repealed.

I will begin my discussion by focusing on the education agenda of the Green Party and then contrast it with the education agenda of the Libertarian Party.

Green Party: Educating Critical and Active Citizens

The 2012 Green Party platform stresses education for active democratic citizenship: "Greens believe every child deserves a public education that fosters critical and holistic thought, and provides the breadth and depth of learning necessary to become an active citizen and a constructive member of our society."[3] In contrast to the 2012 Democratic Party's emphasis on education for work or college and the Republican Party's acceptance of similar human capital goals tempered by nationalistic and moral agenda, the Green Party platform also asserts, "We do not believe our public school system, as it presently operates, helps us reach that goal [education for active citizenship]."[4] In addition, the Green Party rejects part of the agenda of some Republicans by opposing "efforts to restrict the teaching of scientific information and the portrayal of religious belief as fact."[5]

As discussed in Chapters 1 and 2, President Obama's Race to the Top, with its emphasis on education for work or college, is devoid of concern about the education of politically active citizens. Concerns about educating active democratic citizens does not appear in the education agendas of either of the two major political parties which are primarily concerned with educating human capital to benefit the economy and, in the case of Republicans, protecting moral and nationalistic feelings.

The Green Party's concern with educating active citizens can be understood in the context of the Party's concept of democracy, which requires making a distinction between representative government and direct democracy. The democratic aspect of representative government is the right of citizens to vote for their representatives. The Green Party believes that elected representatives limit the ability of citizens to decide important issues. The 1996 Green platform explained it in these words:

> Greens advocate direct democracy as a response to local needs and issues, where all concerned citizens can discuss and decide questions that immediately affect their lives, such as land use, parks, schools and community services. We hold as a "key value" GRASS ROOTS DEMOCRACY and, as such, would decentralize many state functions to the community level and seek expanded roles for neighborhood boards/associations.[6]

The Green platform includes "Grass Roots Democracy" in their list of "10 Key Values" in which the number one on the list of values is: "Every human being deserves a say in the decisions that affect his or her life and should not be subject to the will of another." The 2012 Green platform describes Grass Roots Democracy as:

> Every human being deserves a say in the decisions that affect his or her life and should not be subject to the will of another. Therefore, we will work to increase public participation at every level of government and to ensure that our public representatives are fully accountable to the people who elect them. We will also work to create new types of political organizations which expand the *process of participatory democracy by directly including citizens in the decisionmaking process* [author's emphasis].[7]

In other words, the Green Party envisions schools educating students for maximum participation in the control of their own lives and the governing institutions that affect their lives. Consequently, unlike the education agendas of the two major political parties, the Green Party advocates that schools: "Include a vigorous and engrossing civics curriculum in later elementary and secondary schools, to teach students to be active citizens."[8]

The Green platform statement, "We do not think that schools should turn our children into servile students, employees, consumers or citizens,"[9] is an implicit criticism of human capital goals with its emphasis on the preparation of workers. The Green Party's inclusion of "servile . . . consumers" reflects a historic concern of the Green Party with consumer-capitalism. Consumerism, as I discuss later in this chapter, is a historic concern of the Green Party.

The Green platform is concerned with the increased privatization and corporatization of public schools resulting from No Child Left Behind and the Race to the Top. The 2012 Green platform specifically complained about the involvement of certain foundations in the privatization of public schools:

> We also call attention to the results of a quarter century of corporate funding from the likes of the Bradley and Wal-Mart Family Foundations and a decade of No Child Left Behind—a vast, well-endowed and lucrative sector which seeks to dismantle, privatize, or militarize public education and destroy teachers unions.[10]

The platform criticizes testing and spending on charter schools: "Regimes of high-stakes standardized testing and the wholesale diversion of resources away from public schools are provoking crises for which the bipartisan corporate consensus recommends school closings, dissolution of entire school districts and replacement by unaccountable, profit-based charter schools."[11] Consequently, a recommended action of the 2012 Green platform was: "Oppose the administration of public schools by private, for-profit entities."[12]

The reference to "militarize public education" is in part a reference to No Child Left Behind which opened school records to military recruiters. The 2004 Green platform was more specific: "The Leave No Child Behind Act must be repealed, especially the section that gives the military access to student records."[13] The 2012 platform provides a more expansive condemnation of what the Greens call the militarization of schools:

> We demand an end to the militarization of our schools. JROTC programs are an expensive drain on our limited educational resources and a diversion from their important mission to prepare our young to assume their role in a peaceful tomorrow. ASVAB[14] testing is being used to mine public school student bodies for data to support military recruiting. Forbid military access to student records. The Pentagon's Recruitment Command is misdirecting public tax dollars on manipulative campaigns that prey on our young. We insist that local education authorities stand up to these destructive practices.[15]

Unlike the 2012 Republican and Democratic Parties, which substituted standards and testing for equality of educational opportunity, the 2012 Green platform called for action to: "Eliminate gross inequalities in school funding. Federal policy on education should act principally to provide equal access to a quality education."[16] The proposal for federal policy to ensure equality of education is consistent with previous Green Party statements, such as that of the 2004 Green platform's assertion that: "Federal policy on education should act principally to ensure equal access to a quality education."[17]

The repeated call by the Green Party for equal educational funding might be considered a response to the critics discussed in Chapter 2 who claim that No Child Left Behind and Race to the Top were resulting in increased economic segregation. Also, as discussed in Chapter 1, the call for equal access to quality education parallels President Clinton's efforts in the 1990s to create opportunity to learn standards that would have provided some modicum of effort to provide educational equality.

A striking feature of the 2012 Green Party platform is its dropping of past support for choice within public schools. In the opening to the "Education" section of their 2004 platform it was asserted that: "Greens support educational diversity. We hold no dogma absolute, continually striving for truth in the realm of ideas."[18] Reflecting a view that intellectual diversity is important for social progress, the 2004 platform asserted the importance of school choice:

> Education starts with choice, and within public education we believe in broad choices. Magnet schools, Site-based Management, Schools within Schools, alternative models, and parental involvement are ways in which elementary education can be changed to make a real difference in the lives of our children.[19]

However, the 2004 platform did reject the use of vouchers for privately operated charter schools: "We oppose vouchers, or any scheme that will transfer money out of the public school system ... We also oppose charter schools or the administration of public schools by private, for-profit entities."[20] The 2004 platform asserts that vouchers and privately operated charter schools will result in "a separate and unequal educational system."[21] However, the Green Party has consistently supported home schooling in the context of parental right to control the education of their children.

Green Party: Art Education and Political Activism

A distinguishing feature of the Green Party is promotion of arts education to improve social, environmental, and political conditions. No other political party emphasizes the importance of the arts in improving the quality of society. The wording of the arts section of the Green Party platform has remained the same from 2004 to 2012. It is included in the same part of the platform as education: "E. Education and the Arts." The opening lines of the art section of the 2012 platform expresses the belief that art is important for political empowerment and sustainability of the environment: "Freedom of artistic expression is a fundamental right and a key element in *empowering communities*, and in *moving us toward sustainability* and respect for diversity [author's emphasis]."[22]

There is an important political dimension to this advocacy of arts education. The closest encounter I've had with this linkage between politics and art education is in the writings of Maxine Greene.[23] The statement included in these Green platforms that links art to politics was:

> Artists can create in ways that foster healthy, non-alienating relationships between people and their daily environments, communities, and the Earth. This can include both artists whose themes advocate compassion, nurturance, or cooperation; and artists *whose creations unmask the often-obscure connections between various forms of violence, domination, and oppression, or effectively criticize aspects of the very community that supports their artistic activity* [author's emphasis].[24]

The Green Party includes in the term "art" a wide variety of activities: "Diversity in arts education in the schools including age-specific hands-on activities and appreciative theoretical approaches, exposure to the arts of various cultures and stylistic traditions, and experiences with a variety of media, techniques and contents."[25]

It is through exposure and the practice of different art forms that students learn to see the world in different ways, including breaking through the dominant view of society to lay bare its inner workings and connections. In addition, art is to help students imagine better ways to form political organizations, which results in a form of civic education and social activism.

Thus education in the arts contributes to the overall goal of the Green Party education agenda for a "public education that fosters critical and holistic thought."[26] Holistic thought refers to seeing the world as an interactive system with each part dependent on the other. Thus, protection of the environment is part of a holistic view of the interaction of humans with nature and with the forces of nature interacting with each other. According to the Green Party, arts education contributes to this holistic view: "The integration of the arts and artistic teaching methods into other areas of the curriculum to promote a holistic perspective."[27]

The sharpest contrast between human capital education and the goals of the Green Party can be found in calls for increased funding for STEM (Science, Technology, Engineering, and Mathematics) and the Green Party's call for: "Funding and staffing to incorporate arts education into every school curriculum."[28] For instance, the STEM Education Coalition defines as its central mission "to inform federal and state policymakers on the critical role that STEM education plays in U.S. competitiveness and future economic prosperity and to advocate for policies that will improve STEM education at every level."[29] To achieve this goal, in contrast to the arts goal of the Green Party, the STEM coalition advocates: "Establishing a high-priority for STEM-focused projects, programs, and curricula in education programs that support classroom teaching and learning and out-of-school experiences such as afterschool, co-curricular, and summer programs."[30]

Fundamental differences on social improvement are embodied in the differences between the STEM Education Coalition and the Green Party. The STEM Education Coalition promises that technological progress will solve most of the world's problems. On the other hand, the Green Party sees world progress for humanity as dependent on education for social activism and civic involvement coupled with an arts education that helps students understand the holistic quality of social problems and imagine new solutions. The Green Party does not dismiss technology, but claims that technological development should be considered in a holistic framework that includes the environment, poverty, inequality in wealth, health, the fostering of democratic institutions, and the ability to live a satisfying life.

Green Party: Sustainability and Consumerism

Protecting the environment is a central focus of the Green Party. The Green Party prefaces its education agenda with the statement: "A great challenge facing the people of the United States is to educate ourselves to build a just, *sustainable*, humane and democratic future, and to become responsible and effective citizens of the local and global communities we share [author's emphasis]."[31] The Green Party defines sustainability as achieving a balance between economic growth and protecting the environment. Greens criticize the attitude that nature or the biosphere is something for humans to conquer to serve their own interests rather than recognizing that humans are part of nature and dependent on its existence. The Green platform asserts that both communist and capitalist systems operate to advance economic growth without consideration of the impact on the environment.

> The human community is an element of the Earth community, not the other way around. All human endeavors are situated within the dynamics of the biosphere. If we wish to have sustainable institutions and enterprises, they must fit well with the processes of the Earth. The ideology of industrialism, in both capitalist and communist countries, insists that modern society lives on top of nature and should rightly use and despoil the rest of the natural world as we desire—because any loss of the ecosystems is merely an "externality" in economic thought and because any problems can be

addressed later by a technological fix. We are now living through the painful consequences of that arrogant, ignorant perspective. Many of our children suffer from accumulations of mercury and other toxins in their neurological systems, environmentally related cancer is on the rise, and our air and water are increasingly polluted. Meanwhile, our eco-systems are being compromised by the spreading presence of genetically engineered organisms.[32]

When the Green Party refers to capitalism it is primarily referring to a particular form of capitalism associated with consumerism. In the 2000 presidential election, Ralph Nader, long time consumer advocate, was the Green Party candidate. Nader was the first U.S. presidential candidate to focus on the problems associated with a consumerist ideology. Nader's educational concern was with the impact of consumerist ideology on children and teenagers and what he considered the resulting undermining of democratic activism.

Consumerist ideology assumes that the goal of the economic system is constant growth and consumption of products. Within this framework, the goal of technological development is the production of new goods. However, the production of new goods requires the creation of new human needs. The development of advertising techniques in the U.S. in the early 20th century, and the global spread of these techniques in the 20th and 21st centuries, is the agency for developing these new needs. Economists, such as Simon Patten in the early 20th century, argued that agricultural and industrial development would continually produce surpluses of products. The only way the agricultural and industrial machinery could be maintained, Patten argued, was the creation of new needs.[33] Later, corporations, such as General Motors, introduced the idea of planned obsolescence through advertising new styles and models.

Consequently, advertising not only creates a need for new products but also convinces consumers to abandon products that they own for similar products with different styling. Within the framework of consumerism ideology, personal identity and social status are attached to brand names. People proudly wear clothes with identifying brand names or drive cars that identify their personality or social status.

Working and spending are the central values of consumerist ideology. Constant consumption requires longer hours of work: this is the tragic irony of consumerism. Technological advances do not free people from work but instead make new products that require more work to purchase. For instance, technology could be used to produce durable goods and reduce hours at work.

Commodified leisure, as exemplified by movies, television, Disney World, video games, recreational products, and packaged travel, provide both an escape from work and a reason to work harder. People work harder so that they can buy such items as boats, golf clubs, the newest hiking gear, and tickets for travel on a cruise ship. The desire for commodified leisure fills the fantasy world of the worker. In turn, the consumption of leisure provides escape from the often-numbing quality of office and factory work.

What distinguishes capitalism from consumerism? Capitalism assumes that people make rational choices in a free market, whereas consumerism assumes that individual choices in the market are a result of the manipulation of desires. In turn, political choices are the result of the manipulation of desires through the media. Politicians rely on advertising, media experts, and spin doctors to present their political agenda. Political image takes the place of political substance.

Green Party 2000: Ralph Nader, Consumerism, and Education

During the 2000 presidential campaign, Nader made consumerism the focal point of his educational policy statements. In his acceptance speech as presidential candidate of the Green Party on June 25, 2000, Nader argued that there is a responsibility "to ensure that our children are well cared for. This is an enormous undertaking because our children are now exposed to the most intense marketing onslaught in history."[34] This marketing offensive, Nader argued, involves:

> precise corporate selling ... beamed directly to children separating them from their parents, an unheard of practice formerly, and teaching them how to nag their beleaguered parents as unpaid salesman for companies. There is a bombardment of their impressionable minds.[35]

Nader linked the lack of political activism and concern among youth to the commercialization of their minds. He argued that commodified leisure occupies more and more of children's time. This results, Nader contended, in youth not responding to the growing economic inequalities in the U.S. and between nations. "To the youth of America," Nader warned in his acceptance speech, "beware of being trivialized by the commercial culture that tempts you daily. I hear you saying often that you're not turned on to politics.... If you do not turn on to politics, politics will turn on you."[36]

For Nader, commodified leisure reduced political activity and interfered with the ability of children to learn. Nader argued, "Obviously, you see how our children are not learning enough history, they're not learning how to write. Their attention span is being shrunken by all this entertainment on TV and videos that are beamed to them."[37] In his nomination speech he contended that, "This does not prepare the next generation to become literate, self-renewing, effective citizens for a deliberative democracy."[38]

The problem, as Nader defined it, was corporate targeting of children as present and future consumers. He quoted Mike Searles, former President of Kids-R-Us: "If you own this child at an early age, you can own this child for years to come. Companies are saying, 'Hey, I want to own the kid younger and younger'."[39] To prove his point, he quoted a *Los Angeles Times* interview with Nancy Shalek, President of the Shalek Agency:

> Advertising at its best is making people feel that without their product, you're a loser. Kids are very sensitive to that. . . . You open up emotional vulnerabilities and it's very easy to do with kids because they're the most emotionally vulnerable.[40]

The undermining of parental authority, according to Nader, was the goal of advertisers and their paid child psychologists. Boys and girls under the age of 12, Nader claimed, were responsible for the spending of $25 billion a year. Nader contended that marketers use three methods to "avoid or neutralize parental authority":

> First, they urge the child to nag the parents.
> Second, the sellers take conscious advantage of the absence of parents who are commuting and working long hours away from home.
> Third, the marketers know that if they can undermine the authority, dignity, and judgment of parents in the eyes of their children, the little ones will purchase or demand items regardless of their parents' opinions.[41]

In addition to being disturbed by the undermining of democracy by training of present and future consumers, Nader was disturbed by the effects of advertising and media on the present and future health of children. For instance, he argued that there was a direct link between teenage drinking and car crashes, suicide, date rapes, and problems teenagers have had in school and with their parents. Despite these problems, the alcohol industry advertises to audiences, according to the Federal Trade Commission, that include children and places their products in PG and PG-13 films that appeal to children and teenagers. In addition, the alcohol industry advertised on eight of the 15 television shows that were most popular with adolescents. Advertising led to teenage smoking; for instance, the Marlboro Man, Nader claimed, appealed to teenage desires for independence.[42]

Violence is, Nader contended, presented to children and teenagers through movies, television, and video games. Nader quoted Lt. Col. Grossman, coauthor of *Stop Teaching Our Kids to Kill*, that shooter video games such as Duke Nukem, Time Crisis, and Quake "teach children the motor skills to kill, like military training devices do. And then they turn around and teach them to like it like the military would never do."[43]

Also, according Nader, children's health has been undermined by a "barrage of ads for Whoppers, Happy Meals, Coke, Pepsi, Snickers bars, M&M's, and other junk foods and fast foods."[44] These marketing efforts contribute to the rise of child and teenage obesity and diabetes. Heath risks associated with severe obesity among children, Nader claimed, doubled since the 1960s.

What was Nader's answer to the destruction of democracy through the commercialization of the minds of children and teenagers? First, he argued that Congress should repeal Public Law 96–252, which prohibits the Federal Trade Commission from establishing rules to protect children from commercial advertising. Second, he appealed for a coalition of groups, including conservative organizations, such as the Eagle Forum and Family Research Council, to work for laws to protect children from advertising and limit the access of marketing groups to public schools. Third, he urged citizens to join the Center for a New American Dream, which is dedicated to overthrowing the ideology of consumerism. He recommended that citizens obtain the Center for a New American Dream's pamphlet, "Tips for Parenting in a Commercial Culture."

The Nader campaign also stressed the issue of child poverty, contending that 20 percent of children in the U.S. lived in poverty—a figure much higher than that for any other Western country. In addition, there is a direct link, Nader contended, between childhood poverty and school performance and, consequently, expectations for future earnings. Childhood poverty contributes, Nader argued, to the perpetuation of poverty. Nader called for more expanded health and welfare programs for children that would be paid for out of the future budget surplus of the federal government.

Nader was the first presidential candidate to directly attack the ideology of consumerism and propose an educational agenda that included the protection of children and teenagers from indoctrination into consumerist values. This protection was to be combined with the teaching of an anticonsumerist ideology that included environmental education. In addition, Nader urged government programs to eliminate childhood poverty. The combination of these efforts, Nader believed, would result in a generation dedicated to hands-on participation in democratic processes.

Concern about sustainability and consumerism would continue to be a theme of the Green Party. In the context of education, one goal was to protect students from advertising similar to the issues raised by Nader. For instance, the 2004 Green platform stated: "We are deeply concerned about the intervention in our schools of corporations that promote a culture of consumption and waste. Schools should not be vehicles for commercial advertising."[45] In 2010, the Green platform provided a more abbreviated version about school commercialism: "Prohibit advertising to children in schools. Corporations should not be allowed to use the schools as vehicles for commercial advertising or corporate propaganda."[46] The same wording was used in the 2012 platform. Along with a continued concern about the effect of consumerism of children, the Green Party maintained its dedication to promoting a sustainable environment.

In summary, the Green Party's education agenda is in sharp contrast with the Republican and Democratic Parties. Neither the Democrats nor Republicans include in their agendas the education of active citizens to bring about social change and environmental education for sustainability. In contrast to educating for a holistic view of environmental and social problems and for ways of imagining a better future, the Republican Party retains its traditional concerns with patriotic and character education, including abstinence sex education, and the Democratic Party trumpets Race to the Top as the solution to America's economic problems. Human capital education remains the dominant ideology driving the education concerns of both major political parties, while the Green and, as I will discuss in the next section, Libertarian Parties offer an alternative vision.

The Libertarian Party: Separation of School and State

The Libertarian Party's agenda for education is short, but offers another alternative education vision that is similar, but different, to the Republican Party's concept of educational choice. The single plank in the Libertarian Party's 2012 platform states:

> Education is best provided by the free market, achieving greater quality, accountability and efficiency with more diversity of choice. Recognizing that the education of children is a parental responsibility, we would restore authority to parents to determine the education of their children, without interference from government. Parents should have control of and responsibility for all funds expended for their children's education.[47]

Unlike the Democratic and Republican Parties there is no mention in the Libertarian education agenda of human capital education, educational standards, testing, nationalism, or character education. And unlike the Green Party's emphasis on a holistic vision of the interdependence of humans and nature, the opening lines of the Libertarian 2012 platform emphasizes individualism and personal liberty existing within a free market: "As Libertarians, we seek a world of liberty; a world in which all individuals are sovereign over their own lives and no one is forced to sacrifice his or her values for the benefit of others."[48]

In Chapter 3, I discussed the influence of Friedrich Hayek's free-market thinking on the Republican's support of educational choice, including vouchers and debit cards for use at both public and private schools. However, in general, the Republican Party has not supported a complete free market for education which would turn over all schooling to market forces with all schools operating for profit and dependent for their existence on parental choice. This type of free educational market would allow for any type of curriculum, subject, and teaching method to exist as long as it is supported by parental choice. In other words, if no parent wants a particular curriculum, subject, or teaching method then it will not survive.

Theoretically, an educational free market would remove the control of the ideology of education from politicians. This would mean abolishment of government dictates like the Common Core State Standards and the attempt by state and federal governments to have schools serve the interests of the economy. A free market for education would contribute to a free market of ideas with, at least theoretically, the best ideas surviving. The progress of society would thus be a function of the best ideas that survive the competition of the marketplace.

Concern about the use of schools to push a political agenda appeared in the Western world in the 19th century as the idea of public schooling became popular. Max Stirner (1806–1856) warned that controlling dissemination of ideas through schools was fast becoming central to the governing processes of modern nation-states. Stirner's phrase "wheels in the head" refers to ideas that schools (and now media and information technology) consciously intend to implant in human minds as a means of controlling behavior. These wheels in the head own the individual rather than the individual owning the idea. In his classic volume *The Ego and His Own: The Case of the Individual Against Authority* (1845), Stirner writes about wheels in the head: "The thought is my own only when I have no misgiving about bringing it in danger of death every moment, when I do not have to fear its loss as a loss for me, a loss of me."[49] In other words, public schools were a new instrument of government domination designed to control the thinking and actions of citizens.

In the late 19th century, John Stuart Mill gave voice to a similar idea when he argued that government-operated schools are designed to serve the interests of power by controlling the minds and bodies of citizens. He wrote,

> A general State education is a mere contrivance for molding people to be exactly like one another: and as the mold in which it casts them is that which pleases the predominant power in the government, whether this be a monarch, a priesthood, an aristocracy, or the majority of the existing generation, in proportion as it is efficient and successful, *it establishes a despotism over the mind, leading by natural tendency to one over the body* [author's emphasis].[50]

Reflecting this traditional concern about political control of citizens' minds through public schooling, the Libertarian Party's 2000 platform called for separation of school and state: "We advocate the complete separation of education and State. Government schools lead to the indoctrination of children and interfere with the free choice of individuals."[51] The platform called for ending all government involvement in education: "Government ownership, operation, regulation, and subsidy of schools and colleges should be ended. We call for the repeal of the guarantees of tax-funded, government-provided education, which are found in most state constitutions."[52]

Appeals for separation of school and state continue to be a major theme among Libertarians. For instance, writing on the website Libertarian Solutions, Austin Raynor asserts: "The Need to Abolish Public Education." He writes:

Contrary to general sentiment, we are doing a disservice to our children by continuing to support public education. Markets consistently produce better and more consumer-oriented results than do monopolies or bureaucracies, a rule which applies to schooling just as it does to any other sector. But it is a built-in defense mechanism of the flawed schooling system that it is able to indoctrinate citizens to not question its existence; public schooling itself is the largest propaganda campaign in history. It is a government's dream. But on both a moral and pragmatic basis it must be rejected.[53]

Of course, separation of school and state would mean abolishing compulsory education laws:

Compulsory education is both ineffective and unneeded. Government schools force parents into compromising the values and ideas they want their child to learn. Public schools are sterile institutions that have to focus more on standardizing education to the lowest possible denominator rather than equip our children with the skill to become productive citizens.[54]

While calling for the separation of school and state, the Libertarian Party has suggested indirect funding of schooling through education tax credits during a transition period from a government-controlled public school system to one controlled by parental choice in a free market. Its 2000 legislative agenda stated that the "most important step in the crisis in education is to end government control of education."[55] Recognizing that this will not occur overnight, the Libertarian agenda urged, "We must move toward a system where parents have good, safe, affordable choices for educating their children." To achieve this change in control of education, the Libertarians proposed:

To transfer control of education from bureaucrats to parents and teachers and encourage alternatives to the public school monopoly, the Libertarian Party would:

- support a true market in education – one in which parents and students would not be stuck with a bad local school, because they could choose another;
- implement measures such as tax credits so that parents will have the financial ability to choose among schools;
- provide financial incentives for businesses to help fund schools and for individuals to support students other than their own children;
- eliminate the U.S. Department of Education, which spends billions on education and educates no one. The growth of this agency and its numerous regulations is a major reason for runaway costs in American schools.[56]

Quite different from the Republican support of vouchers and tax credits and the Democrats support of school choice limited to public schools, the Libertarian Party sees education tax credits as a transitional method for moving from government-operated and regulated schools to a complete separation of education and the state.

Conclusion: Saving the Planet and the Education Marketplace

The education agendas of the Green and Libertarian Parties reflect a desire for people to have greater control over their lives. For the Green Party, this control is to result from maximizing participatory or grassroots democracy and educating students for civic activism. For the Libertarian Party, the answer is reducing the role of government and maximizing the role of free markets while separating the school from the state.

Both the Green and Libertarian Parties are concerned about education being an instrument of ideological domination. The Green Party fears that current federal education policies will result in creating servile workers for corporations and passive citizens. The Green Party wants to overcome the use of schools for ideological control by maximizing local control, emphasizing education for civic activism, and expanding art education to unveil social, economic, and political oppression and open the imagination to find new ways of achieving social progress. Libertarians would like to break the bonds of ideological domination by political forces by separating school and state and turning education over to the forces of the marketplace.

The Green Party advocates education for sustainable development and criticizes the growth of consumer capitalism with its throwaway culture and endless quest to produce more products for consumption. Greens particularly criticize advertising targeted at children and advertising in schools.

In contrast, the Libertarians put concerns about the environment in the framework of the free market and limiting government power. Given their desire to separate the school and the state, there are no calls for environmental education. However, from a Libertarian standpoint, environmental education might be something chosen by parents in a free market of schools. The 2012 Libertarian platform states: "We support a clean and healthy environment and sensible use of our natural resources ... *Free markets and property rights stimulate the technological innovations and behavioral changes required to protect our environment and ecosystems* [author's emphasis]."[57]

Both the Green and Libertarian Parties provide important alternatives to the education agendas of the Democratic and Republican Parties. For those objecting to No Child Left Behind and Race to the Top, they might find their ideological soul mates in one of these two political organizations.

Notes

1 Platform 2012 Green Party of the United States, Presented to the Presidential Nominating Convention July 2012, p. 28. Retrieved from http://www.gp.org/committees/platform/2012/ on May 14, 2013.
2 Libertarian Party Platform, as adopted in Convention, May 2012, Las Vegas, Nevada, p. 5. Retrieved from https://www.lp.org/files/LP%20Platform%202012.pdf on May 14, 2013.
3 Platform 2012 Green Party of the United States, p. 27.
4 Ibid., p. 27.
5 Ibid., p. 28.
6 The 1996 Green Platform, "IV. Platform Policy Document: Democracy: B. Political Participation." Retrieved from www.greenparty.org on February 1, 2001.
7 Ibid., p. 5.
8 Ibid., p. 28.
9 Ibid., p. 27.
10 Ibid., p. 27.
11 Ibid., p. 27.
12 Ibid., p. 28.
13 Green Party of the United States, "2004 Platform" as adopted at the National Nominating Convention, Milwaukee, Wisconsin—June, 2004, p. 28. Retrieved from http://www.gp.org/platform/2004/2004platform.pdf on May 16, 2013.
14 The ASVAB is a multiple-aptitude battery that measures developed abilities and helps predict future academic and occupational success in the military. It is administered annually to more than one million military applicants, high school, and post-secondary students. Retrieved from the Official Site of the ASVAB, http://official-asvab.com/ on May 16, 2013.
15 Platform 2012 Green Party of the United States, p. 28.
16 Ibid., p. 28.
17 Ibid., p. 28.
18 Ibid., p. 27.
19 Ibid., p. 27.
20 Ibid., p. 28.
21 Ibid., p. 28.
22 Platform 2012 Green Party of the United States, p. 29.
23 See Maxine Greene, *Releasing the Imagination: Essays on Education, the Arts, and Social Change* (New York: Jossey-Bass, 2000).
24 Platform 2012 Green Party of the United States, p. 29.
25 Ibid., p. 29.
26 Ibid., p. 27.
27 Ibid., p. 29.
28 Ibid., p. 29.
29 STEM Education Coalition, "General Mission," p. 1. Retrieved from http://www.stemedcoalition.org/wp-content/uploads/2010/05/One-pager-on-STEM-Ed-Coalition.pdf on May 16, 2013.
30 Ibid.
31 Ibid., p. 27.
32 Ibid., p. 40.
33 Simon N. Patten, *The New Basis of Civilization* (Cambridge: Harvard University Press, 1968).
34 Ralph Nader, "Children and Education." Retrieved from http://votenader.org/on January 22, 2001.
35 Ibid.

36 Ibid.

37 Ibid.

38 Ibid.

39 Ralph Nader, "Why Is the Government Protecting Corporations That Prey on Kids?" Retrieved from http://votenader.org on September 22, 1999.

40 Ibid.

41 Ralph Nader, "Making Parents Irrelevant." Retrieved from http://votenader.org on October 27, 1999.

42 Nader, "Why Is the Government Protecting Corporations That Prey on Kids?"

43 Ibid.

44 Ibid.

45 Green Party of the United States, "2004 Platform," p. 27.

46 Green Party of the United States Platform 2010 as adopted by the Green National Committee, p. 27. Retrieved from http://www.gp.org/committees/platform/2010/index.php on May 14, 2013.

47 Libertarian Party Platform as adopted in Convention, May 2012, Las Vegas, Nevada, p. 5. Retrieved from http://www.lp.org/platform on April 15, 2013.

48 Ibid., p. 1.

49 Max Stirner, *The Ego and His Own: The Case of the Individual Against Authority,* trans. Steven T. Byington (New York: Libertarian Book Club, 1963), p. 342.

50 John Stuart Mill, *On Liberty* (Indianapolis, IN: The Liberal Arts Press, 1956), p. 129.

51 On the Issues, "Libertarian Party on Education." Retrieved from http://www.ontheissues.org/celeb/Libertarian_Party_Education.htm on May 14, 2013.

52 Ibid.

53 Austin Raynor, "The Need to Abolish Public Education," The Libertarian Solution. Retrieved from http://www.libertariansolution.com/liberty-library/012/the-need-to-abolish-public-education on May 16, 2013.

54 Libertarianism, "Education Overview." Retrieved from http://www.libertarianism.com/content/88/Issues on May 6, 2013.

55 On the Issues, "The Libertarian Party's Legislative Program, Nov 7, 2000." Retrieved from http://www.ontheissues.org/celeb/Libertarian_Party_Education.htm on May 14, 2013.

56 Ibid.

57 Libertarian Party Platform as adopted in Convention, May 2012, p. 4.

6

NEW AGENDA FOR AMERICAN SCHOOLS

In this chapter, I am proposing a New Agenda for American Schools that brings together proposals I have made in other contexts. These proposals include an amendment to the U.S. Constitution, replacing the current human capital paradigm dominating educational policy, and a renewed emphasis on holistic environmental education. My New Agenda for American Schools answers important issues raised by the Green and Libertarian Parties and the criticisms made of the educational agendas of the Democratic and Republican Parties.

Issues Requiring a New Agenda for American Schools

The importance of new directions for American schools can be found in some of the criticisms made by the Green and Libertarian Parties of the Republican and Democratic Parties' education agendas. For instance, both the Green and Libertarian Parties are critical of political imposition of a school curriculum such as the Race to the Top's Common Core State Standards. Both minority political parties are concerned with limiting political control over the minds of students. The Green Party seeks to return schools to local control through participatory democracy. The Libertarian Party would limit the ability of government to impose political ideologies on students through separation of school and state.

The Green Party is particularly critical of the continued existence of inequality of educational opportunity, which both No Child Left Behind and Race to the Top have done little to alleviate. In fact, as discussed in Chapter 2, economic segregation of students has increased and there are few efforts to equalize school funding. The only equality promised by the Common Core State Standards is that all students will study the same curriculum but under differing conditions of funding.

The Green Party is also critical of the increased privatization of schools and the corporatization of education. As discussed in Chapter 2, Race to the Top has increased involvement of for-profit companies selling products and services to schools. Also, Republicans support vouchers and debit cards for purchase of education from private schools. In both cases, public money is channeled into private hands rather than being directly spent to ensure equality of educational opportunity in public schools. On the other hand, the Libertarian Party welcomes privatization with a belief that the free market will ensure equality of educational opportunity.

The human capital paradigm still dominates educational discussions in both the Republican and Democratic Parties despite the lack of longitudinal research proving that education alone, without other government measures related to employment and income distribution, will solve the problems of unemployment and the growing income gap or improve the ability of the U.S. to compete in the global economy. The Green Party does not adopt the human capital rhetoric but believes economic growth should be in the context of environmental sustainability and the abandonment of consumer capitalism. Of course, the Libertarian Party would see a free market of ideas determining educational goals and paradigms.

The Green Party rejects attempts by the government to control social behavior, particularly the efforts of the Republican Party, through the schools. It places the responsibility for character and sexual education in the hands of parents. The 2012 Green Party platform calls for action to: "Encourage parental responsibility by supporting parenting, and increasing opportunities for parents to be as involved as possible in their children's education. Values start with parents. Teaching human sexuality is a parental and school responsibility."[1] Libertarians would make both the support and the determination of values a function of the free market.

In recent times, neither the Republican Party nor Democratic Party call for or express concern about environmental education despite the fact that pollution and climate change are important issues affecting the destiny of humanity. The Green Party calls for education for a sustainable economy within a holistic framework of the interaction between nature and humanity. On the other hand, Libertarians believe that any environmental education programs will result from parental choice in a free market of education.

Given these concerns and the problems caused by Democratic and Republican education agendas, I propose an amendment to the U.S. Constitution to ensure equality of educational spending, limiting the political imposition of ideas, and protection of languages, and cultures. Also, I will argue that we must replace the human capital paradigm with one that stresses that the goal of schooling should be to maximize people's ability to lead long and satisfying lives. And finally, we need a holistic environmental education, which, I would argue, helps humanity have a long and satisfying life.

New Agenda for American Schools: Constitutional Amendment

The U.S. Constitution was written before schooling became an important part of the social fabric. There is nothing in the U.S. Constitution about education and, consequently, the power over schooling has been given to state governments. One result is the inability of the federal government to mandate equal educational funding of public schools. This is highlighted by the ruling on school finance in the U.S. Supreme Court decision in *Rodriguez v. San Antonio School District* (1973). In this case, the U.S. Supreme Court refused to consider the issue of school finance, declaring, "The consideration and initiation of fundamental reforms with respect to state taxation and education are matters reserved for the legislative processes of the various states."[2]

Besides equal financing of education, it is important to protect the academic freedom of teachers to manage their own classrooms without outside interference from political forces. Also, in response to the Republican agenda of "English-Only" and the long history of educational attempts to destroy the languages and cultures of conquered peoples, including Native Americans, Puerto Ricans, Hawaiians, and Mexicans (northern part of Mexico conquered during the Mexican-American war), I would provide constitutional protection for languages and cultures.

I do not intend that my proposed amendment be fixed in stone. Like any other document it should be debated and changed.

Proposed Education Amendment to the U.S. Constitution:

1. Everyone has the right to receive an education.
2. Primary, secondary, and higher education shall be free.
3. Public schools will be equally financed.
4. Primary and secondary education shall be compulsory until the age of 16. The government will ensure, through financial assistance, scholarships, or other means, that no one is denied an education or access to an educational institution because of lack of financial resources including resources for food, shelter, and medical care.
5. Teachers in all government-operated schools will have the academic freedom to choose the methods of instruction and class materials to implement local curriculum requirements.
6. Local communities will have primary control over public school curricula and methods of instruction.
7. Everyone has a right to an education using the medium of their mother-tongue within a government-financed school system when the number of students requesting instruction in that mother-tongue equals the average number of students in a classroom in that government-financed school system.

8. Everyone has the right to learn the dominant or official language of the nation. The government-financed school system will make every effort to ensure that all students are literate in the dominant or official language of the country.

New Agenda for American Schools: Long Life and Happiness

In *A New Paradigm for Global School Systems: Education for Long Life and Happiness*, I proposed a new global educational paradigm as an alternative to the increasingly criticized emphasis on education for economic growth and meeting labor market needs.[3] In this paradigm, educational policy is focused on longevity and subjective well-being (happiness) rather than economic growth and personal income. These two objectives, while taking on different meanings in different cultures and religions, can be measured; they can be given concrete and objective meaning that can be used to guide public policy.

In my proposed goals for schooling, I am focusing on the social conditions that improve the chances of living a long and satisfying life. There is ongoing community health and happiness research that will help achieve these goals. Currently, global educational policy is centered on economic growth and preparing workers for the world's labor market. Economic growth is considered the measure of social progress. But these policies are increasingly criticized because of their negative effects on the quality of life. For instance, Nobel economist Amartya Sen is concerned about development policies that focus solely on economic growth. In *Development As Freedom*, he uses longevity rates as a guide to the quality of human life.[4] Sen stresses that,

> Since life expectancy variations relate to a variety of social opportunities that are central to development (including epidemiological policies, health care, educational facilities and so on), an income-centered view is in serious need of supplementation, in order to have a fuller understanding of the process of development.[5]

International studies of happiness or living a satisfying life find that money is important for the food, shelter, and health care, but any additional money does not necessarily result in increased happiness. On the other hand, extreme inequalities in wealth and the stress of competition seem to contribute to a shorter lifespan and unhappiness.[6] In the context of my proposed educational paradigm, income and jobs remain important for their contribution to longevity and happiness; people need food, shelter, and health care.

Public health studies show that social inequality causes stress for those at the bottom of a hierarchy, which in turn contributes to poor health, a reduced life span, and a low sense of subjective well-being.[7] Stress in humans produces identifiable physical reactions resulting, among other things, in high blood pressure, heart disease, and diabetes. As stress occurs there is a rise in catecholamine, which causes an increase in blood pressure, pulse rate, and a diversion of blood from the intestines. Also, stress increases levels of Glucocorticoid, which increases blood sugar causing a resistance to insulin resulting in the possibility of adult-onset diabetes. There is also a change in fats in the blood causing low levels of HDL (the good cholesterol), increased plasma triglyceride, blood glucose, and high blood pressure resulting in potential heart disease. Simply stated, stress reduces longevity.[8]

How does social inequality cause stress? The answer to this question takes us back to the notion of capabilities or, as stated by Sen, "people's ability to lead the kind of lives they value—and have reason to value."[9] If you are at the bottom of most social hierarchies you have less chance of leading the type of life you value and, consequently, you suffer the physical results of stress. And also, given the structure of most hierarchies such as corporations and government civil services, the "bicycling reaction" occurs, producing more stress.

Bicycling is an important image for understanding the effect of social hierarchies. The bicycle image is that of a person bending forward with hands on the handlebars while kicking back on the pedals. Or, in other words, bowing to authority while abusing those below. There is anger and stress caused by bowing to authority and there is anger and stress caused in subordinates being kicked. Public health authority Richard Wilkinson quotes Volker Sommer, a distinguished primatologist, about how bicycling takes place in the animal world of which humans are a part:

> It is very common in nonhuman primates that they, after having received aggression from a higher ranking individual, will redirect aggression towards lower ranking ones. It can be a real chain reaction: Alpha slaps beta, beta slaps gamma, gamma slaps delta, delta slaps . . . .[10]

Wilkinson summarizes the bicycle reaction among humans: "There is a widespread tendency for those who have been most humiliated, who have had their sense of selfhood most reduced by low social status, to try to regain it by asserting their superiority over any weaker or more vulnerable groups."[11]

In *A New Paradigm for Global School Systems*, I present a possible curriculum and textbook for providing the conditions for teachers and students to have a school experience that enhances their chances of having a long life and having satisfying school and lifetime experiences. I also suggest that the same principles be applied to the work of school teachers. Research suggests that anger about one's job and a lack of control over one's work contributes to a reduced lifespan. In other words, angry teachers do not benefit either teachers or students. Therefore, teachers' working conditions and control over their teaching material are as important for creating satisfying learning experiences for students. In the above mentioned book, I proposed the following:

Guidelines for a Global Core Curriculum

1. The curriculum should contain the knowledge and skills to maximize physical and mental health for living a long and happy life.
2. The curriculum should contain the knowledge and skills needed to maximize a person's capabilities to choose a life they value.
3. The curriculum should contain the knowledge and skills, including knowledge about research on the causal factors influencing longevity and subjective well-being, so that school graduates will be able to actively ensure that environmental, social, political, and economic conditions promote a long and happy life for themselves and all other people.
4. The curriculum should contain knowledge and skills that will create the emotional desire and ethical belief in school graduates that will cause them to actively help others live a long and happy life.[12]

Guidelines for Global Methods of Instruction

1. Instructional methods should avoid increasing social inequalities between students.
2. Methods of instruction should enhance cooperation and trust between students and between students and teachers.
3. Methods of instruction should enhance optimal learning experiences or the joy of learning.[13]

Guidelines for Global School Organization

1. Schools should be organized to reduce the stress caused by the "bicycle syndrome." As part of reducing the effect of the bicycle syndrome, there should be a reduction—elimination would not be possible or necessarily desirable—of social inequalities between administrators, teachers, and students.
2. Principles of trust and cooperation should permeate the school environment.
3. The environmental conditions of the school, including its architectural design, landscaping, and availability of clean air, safe water, and healthy food, should maximize the opportunity for administrators, teachers, and students to live a long and happy life.
4. Whenever possible schools should include physical and mental health facilities that will maximize the health and subjective well-being of administrators, teachers, and students.[14]

New Agenda for American Schools: Environmental Education

Environmental education contributes to long life and happiness by reducing the impact of pollution on people's health and the possibility of increased deaths and injuries from weather conditions caused by global climate change. In addition, natural settings contribute to human happiness as evidenced by the creation and use of parks, pristine natural sites, and the desire by people to hike, swim, and stroll through natural settings.

I agree with the Green Party that there should be a holistic approach to environmental education that demonstrates the interrelationship of humans with nature and humans with humans, along with the impact of economic development on the biosphere. The concept of the biosphere, a key element of environmental education, was introduced by Vladimir Vernadsky's 1926 book *The Biosphere* in which he criticized Western science for trying to understand nature by breaking it down into smaller and smaller parts.[15] Vernadsky caused a revolution in Western science by declaring:

> Basically man cannot be separated from it [biosphere]; it is only now that this indissolubility begins to appear clearly and in precise terms before us . . . Actually no living organism exists on earth in a state of freedom.[16]

Vernadsky asserted, "All organisms are connected indissolubly and uninterruptedly, first of all through nutrition and respiration, with the circumambient material and energetic medium."[17]

Therefore, in *A New Paradigm for Global School Systems*, I propose a global core curriculum that embodies environmental education.

Global Core Curriculum

1. The overarching framework for learning would be a human-centered biosphere.
2. The focus of learning should be on how the biosphere can promote human happiness and longevity.
3. The traditional subjects of the human capital curriculum along with environmental and human rights education would be integrated in holistic lessons that would:
   a. teach students the political, social, and economic conditions that have decreased and increased human life-spans and subjective well-being;
   b. require the use of problem-solving methods, including the use of imagination, to create conditions that promote a long life and happiness;
   c. give students the tools to change the world;
   d. develop the ethical responsibility needed to protect happiness and lives of others.[18]

Conclusion: The Promise of a New Agenda for American Schools

My proposed education agenda is tentative and I hope it will be refined through criticisms and discussions. We do need new thinking about the purposes of public education. There is little evidence that human capital education goals will result in economic growth, reduction in income inequalities, or even make the U.S. stronger in the world economy; these results depend more on government economic policies than schools. The current emphasis on education for work or college neglects preparing students for participation in political institutions or civic activism. Current policies are increasing economic and racial segregation of students while turning school functions over to for-profit corporations.

Hopefully, my proposed constitutional amendment, new paradigm, and holistic environmental education will spark a public debate that will lead to schools serving the interests of the people rather than the economic concerns of corporations.

Notes

1 Platform 2012 Green Party of the United States, Presented to the Presidential Nominating Convention July 2012, p. 28. Retrieved from http://www.gp.org/committees/platform/2012/ on May 14, 2013.
2 Joel Spring, *American Education: An Introduction to Social and Political Aspects* (White Plains, NY: Longman, 1978), p. 228.
3 Joel Spring, *A New Paradigm for Global School Systems: Education for Long Life and Happiness* (Mahwah, NJ: Lawrence Erlbaum Associates, Publishers, 2007).
4 Amartya Sen, *Development As Freedom* (New York: Anchor Books, 2000).
5 Ibid., pp. 46–47.
6 See Spring, *A New Paradigm for Global School Systems*, pp. 37–71.
7 See Ichiro Kawachi and Bruce P. Kennedy in *The Health of Nations: Inequality Is Harmful to Your Health* (New York: The New Press, 2002); Michael Marmot, *The Status Syndrome: How Social Standing Affects Our Health and Longevity* (New York: Henry Holt and Company, 2004); and Richard Wilkinson, *The Impact of Inequality: How to Make Sick Societies Healthier* (New York: The New Press, 2005).
8 Marmot, *The Status Syndrome*, pp. 113–115.
9 Sen, *Development As Freedom*, p. 18.
10 Wilkinson, *The Impact of Inequality*, p. 224.
11 Ibid., p. 225.
12 Spring, *A New Paradigm for Global School Systems*, p. 65.
13 Ibid., p. 66.
14 Ibid., p. 66.
15 Lynton Keith Caldwell, *International Environmental Policy From the Twentieth to the Twenty-First Century: Third Edition* (Durham, NC: Duke University Press, 1996), pp. 24–25.
16 As quoted in Caldwell, *International Environmental Policy from the Twentieth to the Twenty-First Century*, p. 26.
17 Ibid., p. 26.
18 Spring, *A New Paradigm for Global School Systems*, p. 9.

INDEX